REVIVAL

REVIVAL

WHEN

GOD

COMES

TO

CHURCH

STEVE GAINES

B&H
PUBLISHING
BRENTWOOD, TENNESSEE

Published by B&H Publishing Group
Brentwood, Tennessee

Dewey Decimal Classification: 269.2
Subject Heading: REVIVAL \ EVANGELISTIC WORK \
HOLY SPIRIT

Cover design by Molly von Borstel, FaceOut. Tabernacle image
by Steve Creitz/prophecyart. Baptism photo by Steve Rice,
Copyright © 1973, Los Angeles Times. Used with Permission.
Bird photo by Kriengsuk Prasroetsung/Shutterstock. Steeple photo
by why forget photo/Shutterstock. Additional images by Krasovski
Dmitri, kondr.konst, Paladin12, and Ganguli246/Shutterstock.
Author photo by Bellevue Baptist Church staff.

1 2 3 4 5 6 • 27 26 25 24

DEDICATION

I dedicate this book to two men—Roy Fish and Don Miller, both of whom are deceased. God used them to plant a hunger in my heart for revival and prayer. I served as Dr. Fish's grader for seven years at Southwestern Theological Seminary in Fort Worth, Texas. He taught a PhD seminar on "The History of Spiritual Awakenings" that literally changed my life and ministry. As I studied the great awakenings that God has sent to his people over the years, the Lord birthed a hunger for revival deep in my soul. Likewise, Brother Don taught a prayer seminar that I attended my first year in seminary. I invited him to teach that same prayer seminar in all four churches I have pastored. I learned from him about how to commune intimately with the Lord in prayer. He was and still is the greatest prayer-warrior I've ever met. I am forever grateful for both of these godly brothers in Christ. Though they are both in heaven, their legacies of revival and prayer continue to live in the hearts of those they mentored for decades.

ACKNOWLEDGMENTS

I am grateful for the many people who helped in various ways with the publication of *Revival: When God Comes to Church*. Thank you, Donna, for being my wife since 1980 and for pursuing the Lord so beautifully. You are the most Christlike person I know. You live in revival every day. Thank you, pastors Josh Smith and Steve Smith, for encouraging me to write this book. I know you both have a heart for revival. Thank you, Ben Mandrell, CEO of Lifeway Christian Resources for being willing to publish the book. Thank you, Matthew Hawkins and your team at B&H, for all the encouragement and help. Thank you to my administrative assistant, Candy Phillips, for proofreading the manuscript. Thank you, Noah Sidhom, for all your help and advice. You're one of the brightest and most godly people I know. And thank you to my longtime, best friends, Bill Street, David Jett, and Russ Quinn for seeking the Lord and diligently praying for revival for decades. You guys are my heroes. May we live to see the glory of God fill the house of God again! "O Lord, open the windows of heaven and come down!"

"Will you not revive us again
so that your people
may rejoice in you?"
Psalm 85:6

"Lᴏʀᴅ, I have heard the report about you;
Lᴏʀᴅ, I stand in awe of your deeds.
Revive your work in these years;
make it known in these years.
In your wrath remember mercy!"
Habakkuk 3:2

CONTENTS

INTRODUCTION

I grew up in a relatively small, Southern Baptist church located in a county seat town in West Tennessee. The pastor was a kind, Christlike man. The deacons were servants, the teachers were kind and knowledgeable, the choir sang beautifully, and we had a good youth ministry. My father was a deacon and the head of the ushers. My mother taught children's Sunday school. We were very involved in that church.

But when I was a sophomore in high school, I turned away from the Lord and the church. I was a pretty good football player on a successful team. I started running with some of my teammates who liked to drink and party. As a result, for most of the next three years, until the spring of my freshman year in college, I lived a sinful life. It wasn't my church's fault, my parents' fault, or anyone else's fault. It was all my fault.

But I've often wondered whether or not I would have strayed if I had known more Christians like the ones I read about in the book of Acts.

What should a church of the Lord Jesus Christ look like in the twenty-first century? Should it resemble the culture around it? Or should it look like the earliest church in the book of Acts?

Can a church faithfully share the gospel of Jesus Christ with non-Christians while simultaneously seeking to appease our secular culture? Is it possible for Christians today to be true to the gospel of Jesus while they remain worldly?

The gospel of Jesus not only differs from our worldly culture; it is an outright affront to it. The gospel states forthrightly that all people are sinners by nature and by choice. Consequently, we are separated from God and in need of salvation. Apart from a relationship with Jesus Christ, there is no hope for forgiveness of sin and peace with God. People need to be regenerated. For that to happen, they must *repent* and turn from their sins, *believe* savingly in Jesus's atoning death and bodily resurrection, and volitionally *receive* Jesus Christ as their Lord and Savior. After someone becomes a Christian, God commands him to leave his worldly ways and live a holy, Christlike life. He must adhere to biblical doctrine that will go against the beliefs of our culture. Indeed, Christians are to be different from the world.

I enjoy the tune of Louis Armstrong's renowned song "It's a Wonderful World," but I disagree with the lyrics. It's true that the world God originally created was "wonderful" before sin entered it. But after Eve and Adam ate that forbidden fruit in the garden of Eden, the world changed drastically. Their sin caused our world to come under the curse of God. Because our world is cursed, it will never function correctly until Christ returns and reigns as King of kings. Thus, Christians should embrace the amazing example of Jesus and the earliest Christians.

Again, whenever I look at Acts, I can't help but think, *Why don't our churches today look like that?* I once heard someone say,

"It's time for churches to stop focusing on the book of *Numbers* and start focusing on the book of *Acts*!" That clever rhetoric of course is not a dismissal of the actual Old Testament book of Numbers but a call to check our pragmatic quest for church attendance with a pursuit of the Holy Spirit.

J. B. Phillips, the Anglican clergyman who paraphrased the New Testament in the 1950s, wrote a stunning preface when his first edition of Acts came onto the market. He got honest about how his work had impacted him.

> It is impossible to spend several months in close study of [this] remarkable short book . . . without being profoundly stirred and, to be honest, disturbed. The reader is stunned because he is seeing Christianity, the real thing, in action for the first time in human history. The newborn Church, as vulnerable as any human child, having neither money, influence, nor power in the ordinary sense, is setting forth joyfully and courageously to win the pagan world for God through Christ. The young church, like all young creatures, is appealing in its simplicity and singleheartedness. . . .
>
> Yet we cannot help feeling disturbed as well as moved, for this surely is the Church as it was meant to be. It is vigorous and flexible, for these are the days before it ever became fat and short of breath through prosperity, or muscle-bound

by over-organization. These men did not make "acts of faith," they believed; they did not "say their prayers," they really prayed. They did not hold conferences on psychosomatic medicine, they simply healed the sick. But if they were uncomplicated and naïve by modern standards, we have ruefully to admit that they were open on the Godward side in a way that is almost unknown today.[1]

Our churches today could look more like *that* church. That's why I have written this book. The church in the book of Acts was known for following the Lord Himself with every step they took. They had the anointing of the Holy Spirit and the presence of Jesus Christ.

When God's manifest presence comes to a fellowship of believers in Christ, God's people experience revival. I'll address what revival is and isn't in chapter 1, but my favorite way to define revival is, simply, *when God comes to church.* The Lord Himself is the answer for all our problems. We don't need another program; we need His presence. We don't need better personalities in the spotlight; we need His presence. We don't need slick marketing; we need His presence. Lights, cameras, and websites don't matter as much as the presence and power of God. The Holy Spirit is our primary draw. When He touches people, they're never the same.

Some might object and say, "Well, Acts was a special case and time. God gave them special power to get the church up and rolling. He doesn't do that in our day." Frankly, I disagree. Why would God put us on earth at this point in history and withhold from us the same power He gave to the earliest Christians? Our modern culture is just as evil and sinful, if not more so, than the one they faced. God wants to redeem people today just as He did then.

Most people recognize that our nation and world are in serious trouble morally and spiritually. I'm convinced we are long past a political, secular, or social solution. We dare not look primarily to Republicans or Democrats to repair our broken land. If that were possible, our nation would have already been repaired. But we all know that hasn't happened. Secular social improvements are unable to channel the tide of culture in the right direction.

What our world needs is a heaven-sent revival among the followers of Jesus Christ. In *Revival: When God Comes to Church*, I invite you to join me as we analyze and imagine how our churches today can look like the church of the first century. Infused with the Holy Spirit, early believers evangelized most of the known world within only three centuries. When Christians are reignited with the flame of the Holy Spirit and begin to take the gospel of Jesus to our secular, lost, and hurting culture, real change will come. Our communities are spiritually sick and dying. The Lord's presence among His people in His churches is the answer to our problems. I encourage you to read the following pages with an open heart and a prayerful attitude. Time is of the essence. It's time for revival.

Chapter 1

WHO'S IN THE HOUSE?

Since 1978, I have served on the staff of several Baptist churches. In one of those churches, on a Wednesday night, our congregation gathered for prayer. We prayed for our upcoming revival meeting. We prayed for lost people to show up and be saved and for Christians to show up and be revived. Someone asked, "Is there anything else we should pray about?" I raised my hand and said, "Let's pray that God will show up." You could have heard a pin drop.

I wasn't trying to be a smart aleck. I know that God is omnipresent—He is everywhere, simultaneously. But I'd been in a few Christian meetings where God's presence was undeniably manifest. I'd experienced that in student gatherings at the University of Tennessee at Martin, where I attended my first two years of college on a football scholarship. I attended the Fellowship of Christian Athletes meetings. In February 1976, I went with some teammates to a revival meeting at a small, rural Baptist church, and the pastor, Bill Coleman, led me to faith in Christ.

When that happened, I began to avidly read my Bible, pray, attend church, fellowship with other believers, and witness to lost people. In our campus Bible studies, we were often eclipsed by God's presence. That's what I desired for our revival meeting, but it was not to be.

When our revival services came, people attended, sang, prayed, and gave offerings. Sermons were preached, a few were saved (mostly children), and some others rededicated their lives to Christ. But it wasn't what I'd describe as corporate revival. After it was over, someone asked, "Why didn't more happen at our revival meeting?" In frustration, I wanted to say, "Because God didn't show up!" Then I thought, *As a pastor, I want to lead God's people to hunger for His presence more than anything else!*

For more than forty years, I've been a senior pastor, and I've served in leadership in my denomination. I've developed and (hopefully) matured. But one thing hasn't changed: I still want God to show up! I still believe the main thing isn't how many people show up but how much of God's presence shows up.

Revival is more than a feeling. I'm talking about something *real*, like what we read about in the Old Testament when the new temple was dedicated. "The temple, the LORD's temple, was filled with a cloud. And because of the cloud, the priests were not able to continue ministering, for the glory of the LORD filled God's temple" (2 Chron. 5:13–14). That's a great way to define revival: when *the glory of God fills the house of God.*

What do we mean by *revival* or *spiritual awakening*? I once heard evangelist and revivalist Richard Owen Roberts say, "Revival [is] an extraordinary movement of the Holy Spirit producing extraordinary results." He stressed that revival is extraordinary (i.e., not the norm), revival comes from God (not man), and revival produces amazing results.

In a class I took at Southwestern Baptist Theological Seminary, the late Dr. Roy Fish defined *revival* as "an infusion of divine life into the body of Christ which enables the body to love unconditionally, rejoice exceedingly, serve productively, live victoriously, praise appropriately, minister freely, and witness effectively." Dr. Fish was saying that when revival comes, God's people will be aware of His presence, be characterized by life and enthusiasm, love one another and also non-Christians, rejoice and give thanks, serve others, be set free from sinful strongholds as they walk in victory, worship God according to Scripture, be led by the Spirit as they minister, and share the gospel with the lost.

"Revival is when the glory of God (i.e., His manifest presence) fills the house of God and the people of God!" In other words, revival is *when God comes to church* (hence, the title of this book!).

In Acts, some Christians held a prayer meeting and poured out their hearts to God. Then, "the place where they were assembled was shaken, and they were all filled with the Holy Spirit and began to speak the word of God boldly" (Acts 4:31). They had no buildings, but they had God's presence. Some of our churches today could use some spiritual shaking. We need the Holy Spirit to shake out our sin, pride, and satisfaction with church as usual.

Through the years I've seen glimpses of revival. One Sunday at West Jackson Baptist Church in Jackson, Tennessee, when the choir began their special music, I can only say, "God walked into the room." You could sense His presence. People stood and worshipped the Lord. Others knelt at the altar and prayed. Lost people were saved. Christians were blessed. It was a touch of heaven on earth, and we all left wanting more!

I also experienced multiple heavenly invasions during a fourteen-year pastorate at First Baptist Church, Gardendale, Alabama. In the mid-1990s, many people in our church began to pray, fast, and seek the Lord's presence. God blessed our worship services with His manifest presence for several years. Many people were saved and baptized. God moved miraculously.

Since 2005, I've served as the pastor of Bellevue Baptist Church in Memphis. In every worship service, we praise the Lord with worshipful singing, I preach through a biblical text, and then we extend an altar call. People get saved, schedule their baptism, and begin the process of joining our church. We counsel and pray with people about various needs. We also anoint people with oil and pray for them to be healed (cf. James 5:14–16). Not all are healed physically, but we keep praying because God can heal through medicine, miracle, or both. It's our job to pray, and it's God's job to answer however He pleases. In it all, God reminds us that He is in His house!

The Real Quest

Today, many churches seem explainable. Some "grow" simply because they are "well-oiled machines." Many modern worship services seem more like a manufactured performance than a preparation of soil anticipating the Lord's presence. The size and professional polish of a church won't change a person's life. Only the Lord's presence can cause people to stop stealing, stop viewing pornography, and stop abusing others. Yet, in many churches, the motto seems to be: *Come as you are; leave as you came.* People walk out as they came in, except for a bag of church stuff under their arms. Where's the manifest presence of Christ?

Jesus said to the Samaritan woman at the well, "But an hour is coming, and is now here, when the true worshipers will worship the Father in Spirit and in truth. Yes, *the Father wants such people to worship him*" (John 4:23, emphasis added). I like to envision God hovering over Memphis asking, "What church wants to worship Me? I'm seeking My people who possess humble, hungry, holy hearts, who want to jettison their busyness and reach out to Me!"

It doesn't have to be a Baptist church. It just needs to be a church that loves Jesus, the Bible and people, and is willing to pursue God. A church shouldn't be built on personalities or programs. A church should be built on God's presence. In that kind of church, at least *some* things happen that can only be explained by God's presence. If the Holy Spirit moved out, it would all implode!

When a lost man walks into a church that is saturated in prayer, and he sits among people who pursue God, and God's presence is so real he can't deny it, that man is going to say, like the visitors to the Corinthian church, "God is really among you" (1 Cor. 14:25).

Time for Another Awakening

In the book of Acts, thousands of people were saved and whole cities were transformed by God's power. That's what I want to see happen in our day. I want others to experience what I studied in seminary:

- the revivals of Jonathan Edwards, George Whitefield, and John and Charles Wesley in the 1700s,
- the Prayer Meeting Revival of the 1800s,
- the awakenings in Wales and elsewhere in the early 1900s, and
- the Jesus Movement of the late 1960s and early 1970s.

I'm weary of reading about such things because I so desire revival in *our* time so that "seasons of refreshing may come from the presence of the Lord" (Acts 3:20). Yes, we should love God with our *mind* and *strength*, but let's not forget our *heart* and *soul* (cf. Mark 12:30)! My mentor, Roy Fish, used to say, "Your theology can be as straight as a gun barrel but just as empty!"

In the 1500s, the church experienced reformations of our view of the Word, thanks to Luther, Calvin, Zwingli, Knox, and the others who brought us out of the bondage of the Dark Ages. What we need today is a *reformation of worship*—a renewed scriptural understanding of what it means to draw close to God. When we worship, we give the Lord our heart, and He shares His heart with us. What a glorious exchange!

I long to be part of a spiritual awakening in America. I don't believe God is ready to give up on our nation. If God sent a nationwide revival to our country, the evangelistic harvest of souls would be mind-boggling, and the worldwide evangelistic and social effects would last for a hundred years or more. That's why I pray that the Christians in our country will repent and seek God's presence.

Some talk about getting God back into our government and public schools. I want to get God back *into our churches*. When Jesus knocked at a door in Revelation 3:20, He was trying to enter the door of the church of Laodicea, not the door of a human heart. The imagery expresses the Laodicean believers had locked Jesus out of His own church. When Jesus is welcomed back into His churches, everyone—Christians and the world alike—will see an amazing difference.

A Football Revival

In my tenth-grade year, I was on the high school football team in my hometown of Dyersburg, Tennessee. Our school hadn't had a winning team in years. A tough, no-nonsense coach was brought in to make us winners. We practiced hard, but when the season opened, we lost two of our first three games.

That was when our coach had a heart-to-heart talk with us. Standing by the goalpost, he said: "Men, no one around here thinks we can win. Most of you don't think we can win. But the fact is, we *can* win. But we're going to have to pull together, become a team, work harder, and start seeing ourselves as *winners!*"

Something wonderful started under that goalpost. We won seven of our next eight games, finishing the season at 8–3. The next season we went 10–1! The crowds at our games grew exponentially. My senior year we had ten more victories and even went to the state playoffs in Nashville! When the dust settled, we were ranked third in the state. We were the talk of West Tennessee.

You might say our team and my hometown had a "football revival." I had the joy and privilege of playing on three winning teams, and I saw a town come together with pride and joy. And it all started under that goalpost when a few "believers" latched on to a fragile and nearly illusive dream. We wanted to win, and we were willing to do whatever it took to see our dream become a reality. Of course, a winning football season isn't nearly as important as a movement of the Holy Spirit. So my question, as you read this book, is, How much do we desire a profound movement of the Holy Spirit?

In America, for the past six decades, Christian churches and denominations have experienced significant decline. The culture has kicked God out of our public schools. From 1973 to 2022, millions of babies were slaughtered by abortion. Gratefully in 2022, *Roe vs. Wade* was overturned. At the writing of this book, the abortion policy battle is in the hands of state legislatures, making for a chaotic national situation. Also, the LGBTQ culture came "out of the closet" and legalized same-sex "marriage." Sexually transmitted diseases, divorce, teenage pregnancies, anxiety, depression, and suicides are pervasive. We can't build prisons fast enough or large enough to house all the criminals. And our state governments are propped up by the greedy gambling industries. Our problems as a nation seem to go on and on.

What's the answer? Revival! God's Word still says: "[If] my people, who bear my name, humble themselves, pray and seek my face, and turn from their evil ways, then I will hear from heaven, forgive their sin, and heal their land" (2 Chron. 7:14). That was not just a promise for ancient Israel. The Old Testament was written to encourage and instruct Christians of all ages (cf. Rom. 15:4; 1 Cor. 10:11). Christians *are* the people of God today. God's people, not unbelievers, are the ones holding back revival.

God desires to return to His people and to His houses of worship. He is graciously knocking on the doors of our churches.

Will we let God back into His house?

The remainder of this book offers reflections on key components of revival. In chapters 2–3, we'll begin by setting the context for our conversation. I'll follow with a look at some of the accounts of God's presence in the Old Testament and the New Testament in chapters 4–5. Chapters 6–7 provide a historic survey of revivals in America. Then, chapters 8–14 offer practical guidance for pastors and local churches desiring to prepare the hearts of their congregations. Last, chapter 15 addresses some enemies of revival before we close with a vision for the future in chapter 16.

Chapter 2

CHURCH IS NOT A PERFORMANCE

A church building is not a theater. It's not a place where actors perform. A worship center might look like a theater. There's a platform with a choir or praise band leading worship as they face the congregation. There are pews/seats facing in the opposite direction of the people up front. It might look like a performance setting, but it's not. The true focus in any worship service is God Himself, not the congregation. Everyone present—pastors, musicians, and all the congregants are ministering to the Lord in worship. He is the primary audience.

The Christians in the sanctuary are not there to be entertained or to critique the music or the message. Their primary purpose is to worship the Lord. Congregants who complain about the temperature in the sanctuary, the volume of the music or the length of the sermon shouldn't be surprised when their children don't desire to be part of the church when they grow up.

What if people today had to listen to the apostle Peter, who never went to seminary? The early Christian worshippers had no sound technician to amplify sound or reduced echoes. Nowadays, many expect quality performances in the house of God. While most all of us appreciate good lighting, quality sound, pleasant temperatures, and other creature comforts in a worship service, the main thing is to seek the Lord Himself.

If a church isn't focused on worshipping Jesus Christ, a performance mindset can kick in. That's especially true if a congregation airs its services through media outlets. Now it's not just the live audience that must be pleased but also viewers watching on TV or online. If they don't like what they see and hear, they can easily click to a different channel. The media tail can end up wagging the whole dog. Is that really what God intended worship to be?

"Us," "Them," or Him?

Worshipping the Lord was never meant to be showtime. Much of what churches call "worship" today is horizontally focused. We concentrate on pleasing people instead of ministering to God. We're not worshipping vertically, looking up to God.

When we make worship services about us, God notices. We say we're worshipping the Lord, but our minds ask: "How is this coming across? Is everybody happy with the music and the sermon? Are we sticking to the schedule so we won't get out late?" If we're not careful, it can degenerate and become human centered.

Allow me to share a personal core conviction: Worship services should not be designed to attract people. They should be designed to attract the manifest presence of God. And when God's presence shows up, He will attract the people. Numerical growth in the church must never be the goal. We gather to praise and please Jesus, not people! To put it another way: don't seek pragmatic results. Seek Jesus, and He'll give you results in the form of spiritual fruit. The Lord is the true audience; the congregation isn't. Go after God and His blessings will follow.

It's easier to seek people than it is to seek God. We can see people, but we can't see God. But Jesus said the greatest commandment is to love God (cf. Matt. 22:34–40). The second greatest commandment is to love people. In corporate worship, God must come first. As Christians, we should love and worship God *before* we seek to reach out to people. We must minister vertically to God in worship before we minister horizontally to people.

That requires a mental shift. It's not the normal way of thinking. We naturally seek approval from our peers. Instead of asking, *What will people think?* we must ask, *What is God thinking?* I enjoy Christian music, especially contemporary praise music that speaks *to* God, not just *about* him. Songs like . . .

> So when I fight, I'll fight on my knees, with my hands lifted high, oh God, the battle belongs to You! And every fear I lay at Your feet, I'll sing through the night, Oh God, the battle belongs to You![2]

19

O God, my God, I need You; O God, my God,
I need You now! How I need You now! O Rock,
O Rock of ages, I'm standing on Your faithful-
ness! On Your faithfulness![3]

To be sure, songs *about* God and His attributes are good. But addressing God directly seems more intimate. It brings us near to the Lord. All worship music is supposed to draw us close to God. Our preaching also needs to focus on the Lord and what He wants to communicate to a particular congregation at a moment in time. Preaching is not fancy oratory. The preacher isn't seeking to win an elocution contest. We'll discuss more about preaching in chapter 13, but the point is to speak and hear what the Spirit is saying to the church.

Searching for More

Much of my passion for God's presence goes back to the mid-1990s. I was in my thirties and served as the pastor of First Baptist Church, Gardendale, Alabama. Things were going well. People were being saved and joining our church. But I was tired. I wasn't tired *of* ministry, but I was tired *in* the ministry. Then I read *The Transforming Power of Fasting and Prayer* by Bill Bright (founder of Campus Crusade for Christ) . He followed the Lord in a forty-day fast, and it made a remarkable difference in his ministry. A pastor friend of mine in Arkansas had done the same thing.

I decided to follow their lead. I consumed only liquids as I sought the Lord. After several days, I didn't care about food. My intimacy with God went into warp speed. God's Word burned in my heart as I devoured it. I couldn't read the Bible enough, and I couldn't praise the Lord enough.

As Jesus taught, I didn't speak about my fast to others, at least at the beginning. But people could see I was losing weight and asked what was going on. I told them I was seeking God, and fasting was an aid to that. Several joined me. Some opted for twenty-one days; others, ten days, three days, or even just one day.

Almost immediately, our Sunday services changed. I remember a Sunday in the fall of 1996 when we were worshipping, and suddenly, "God was in the house." As I was about to start the sermon, the Lord impressed me to invite people to accept Christ as Savior before I preached. I prayed silently, "Lord, we don't do that here." I sensed Him say, "You do now." I gave the invitation and several gave their lives to Christ. I preached my sermon, extended another invitation, and more people were saved. The same thing happened in our next service. People were saved before and after I preached. God showed up and blessed.

Our attendance began to swell. Newcomers came from all around. We doubled in worship attendance over the next few years and had to start a third worship service, build new buildings and new parking lots. Baptisms soared, people were transformed, and God was glorified.

We had no program strategy and no church-growth plan. Fellow pastors asked me, "What's causing all this?" I'd reply, "It's not a 'what' but a 'who.' God's doing this! We're just going after God." There was no fanaticism[4] and nothing unbiblical, just a fresh move of God. We were in over our heads, but God felt more present than we could have imagined.

The mayor told us that our church was the best PR Gardendale had. Our TV broadcast became a Sunday morning favorite throughout central Alabama. People saw that God was moving and drove to our church to be part of it. Some even moved to Gardendale so they could join the church.

When I interviewed with the pastor search committee at Bellevue in 2005, I said, "I *don't* have a preplanned program. If I come as your next pastor, I won't bring a growth strategy. We'll just go after God and invite the people to come along with us. It's simple but it works." They smiled and said, "We think you're right on track. We don't want a performer. Just bring a heart for God and for the congregation, and we'll back you all the way."

The Lord has blessed the church since we came to Bellevue in 2005. Many have been converted to Christ, and many are attending our worship services on Sundays. We plant and water, and the Lord gives the increase (cf. 1 Cor. 3:6). But the greatest part of all is that our people sense the anointing of God's presence during the musical praise, the preaching, and the altar calls.

Human eloquence and programming won't get the job done in our churches. The supernatural element is essential. Today, most people don't come to church to be entertained. They already live in a multimedia world that can entertain better than the church. They're looking for something Hollywood can't

22

provide—God's presence! The world can outsing, outspeak, and outperform the church, but they can't "out-God" us.

A Different Mindset

It's hard for some church people to shift gears. We've put on religious programs for so long we might feel awkward about changing. But I'm convinced we need to think differently about worship in our churches. Many Christian worship leaders are highly trained, but "concert mode" isn't the same as "worship mode." In church, the musician's job is to lead the people to worship the Lord, not to put on a show. Choirs and soloists must undergo the same paradigm shift. They must minister not for human applause but to usher others into the Lord's presence. Music is not an end in itself; it is only a means. In God's house, there must be only one focus—Jesus! We're to worship and pay full attention to Him. He alone deserves the spotlight. For many, that is a significant shift.

Dead or Alive?

Unless we make this kind of shift, we're left on our own to keep the church alive. We have to brainstorm every week and lean on our own creativity, as the population gets harder and harder to impress.

I once preached a sermon series on the seven churches of Revelation. When I got to the church at Sardis, I zeroed in on Jesus's rather blunt summary: "I know your works; you have a reputation for being alive, but you are dead. Be alert and strengthen what remains, which is about to die, for I have not found your works complete before my God" (Rev. 3:1–2).

I heard of a man who went fishing, and he caught a large snapping turtle. The turtle clamped down on the bait so hard the man couldn't get it off the hook. He had to cut the turtle's head off to reset his fishing line. He threw the dead turtle over into the grass. But in a few minutes, he saw that decapitated turtle walking out of the grass back toward the water. *It was dead and didn't even know it!*

Some churches and churchgoers are like that. They're spiritually dead but still going through religious motions. There's no life of the Spirit within. Like the church at Sardis, they're running on autopilot, and they'll soon crumble into a heap if they don't "wake up." The church of Sardis needed what we need today: a passion for God's presence. Programs and performances won't keep us alive. Only the Lord can do that.

I don't know about you, but I want every Bible-believing, Christ-honoring church in America to leave performance mode and start seeking God's presence. It's time to jettison performance mode and start praying, fasting, repenting, and preaching God's truth. America doesn't need church performances with pretty songs and sermons. We've had enough of that. America needs God's presence and power in our churches. Is that what you're hungry and thirsty for?

Church isn't about human performance. It's about seeking God's power and presence.

Chapter 3

AN AUDIENCE OF ONE

Over the years I've tried an experiment with congregations. I'd say, "On three, everyone say your name out loud. One—two—three—." The result was verbal chaos. Then I'd say, "Now, on three, everyone say, 'Jesus.' One—two—three—*JESUS!*" The previous chaos became coherent because we were unified. I would then explain, "When we focus on ourselves and what we want, church becomes selfish and chaotic. But when we focus on Jesus, He brings harmony."

A worship service should focus primarily on the Lord. It can be *seeker friendly* as long as it is primarily *Savior focused*. We pray and sing to *Jesus*. We preach about *Jesus*. Then we invite people to come to *Jesus*. A biblical worship service should be mainly about *Jesus*.

Focusing on Jesus helps unify the church. When we're Jesus focused, we also align ourselves harmoniously with one another. Consider this: How would you tune an entire showroom of pianos? You wouldn't tune piano 2 with piano 1, then piano 3 with

2, and so on down the line. Each time you tuned another piano, it would get a little more out of tune. By the time you reached piano 20, none of the pianos would be in harmony with one another. BUT, if you tuned *all* the pianos to one central tuning fork, each piano would be on the same pitch because the standard would be constant. A church experiences unity only when we all focus on Jesus, not individual agendas.

More Than Just "Showing Up"

In corporate worship, each church member should intentionally engage with the Lord. You shouldn't just show up, warm a pew, give an offering, listen to the sermon, and go home. In all of it, your goal is to connect with God!

A sports team with lots of talent can lose if they don't "show up" mentally because they wrongly assume the trophy is already theirs. Going through the motions won't cut it. When the clock hits 00:00, they'll be eliminated. Likewise, Christians must do more than "show up" at church. We should pray in advance and prepare ourselves for worship. If we spent as much time preparing our spirits as we do fixing our outfits and hair, we could have revival!

Real worship is ministering to God. Rather than asking one another after a church service, "Did you enjoy church today?" we should ask, "Do you think God was pleased with our worship service today?" What are Sunday mornings like for God? When He looks at our hearts, is He drawn to what He sees? Or does He repeat His words to Isaiah, "These people approach me with their speeches to honor me with lip-service, yet their hearts are far from me, and human rules direct their worship of me" (Isa. 29:13)? Does God enjoy your worship?

The Trap of "Whatever Works"

Too many churches and pastors are looking for a new program to jazz up their church. If church life is just a collection of busy programming, we will all grow weary of it. If church life revolves around programs, the question becomes, Does it work? That's pagan pragmatism, and it's a curse on any church. We must draw near to God to receive His life and power. If we do that, results will take care of themselves. God's work requires God's power, and God's power comes with God's presence. God's work is, "Not by strength or by might, but by [His] Spirit" (Zech. 4:6).

"The Heart of Worship" is a Christian worship song written in 1999 by a British worship leader named Matt Redman. Not everyone knows what triggered it. Matt explains it in his book, *The Unquenchable Worshipper*:

> Some of the things we thought were helping us in our worship were actually hindering us. They were throwing us off the scent of what it means to really worship. We had always set aside lots of time in our meetings for worshipping God through music. But it began to dawn on us that we'd lost something. The fire that

used to characterize our worship had somehow grown cold. In some ways, everything looked great. We had some wonderful musicians, and a good quality sound system. There were lots of new songs coming through, too. But somehow we'd started to rely on these things a little too much, and they'd become distractions. Where once people would enter in [to worship God] no matter what, we'd now wait to see what the band was like first, how good the sound was, or whether we were "into" the songs chosen.

Mike, the pastor, decided on a pretty drastic course of action: we'd strip everything away for a season, just to see where our hearts were. So the very next Sunday when we turned up for church, there was no sound system to be seen, and no band to lead us. The new approach was simple—we weren't going to lean so hard on those outward things anymore. Mike would say, "When you come through the doors of the church on Sunday, what are you bringing as your offering to God? What are you going to sacrifice today?"

If I'm honest, at first I was pretty offended by the whole thing. The worship was my job! But as God softened my heart, I started to see His wisdom all over these actions. At first the meetings were a bit awkward: there were long periods of silence, and there wasn't too much singing going on. But we soon began to learn how to bring heart offerings to God without any external trappings we'd grown used to. Stripping everything away, we slowly started to rediscover the heart of worship.

After a while, the worship band and the sound system re-appeared, but now it was different. The songs of our heart had caught up with the songs of our lips.

Out of this season, I reflected on where we had come as a church, and wrote this song:

> *When the music fades, all is stripped away,*
> *And I simply come;*
> *Longing just to bring something that's of worth*
> *That will bless your heart.*
>
> *I'll bring you more than a song, for a song in*
> *   itself*
> *Is not what You have required.*
> *You search much deeper within through the*
> *   way things appear;*
> *You're looking into my heart.*
>
> *I'm coming back to the heart of worship,*
> *And it's all about You, all about You, Jesus.*
> *I'm sorry, Lord, for the thing I've made it,*
> *When it's all about You, all about You, Jesus.*[5]

The audience of One is looking for more than a thing, a performance, or a song. He's looking for a genuine love relationship. When we move from our church plans and programs and seek His presence, He welcomes us. And people are pulled toward Him as with a magnet.

Letting Jesus Lead

People have asked me over the years, "What's it like to pastor a church in revival?" I've answered, "It's like riding a Brahma bull in a rodeo. You're on top, but you're not in charge!" Indeed, Jesus is the Head of the church, and He has the right to lead us any way He chooses. We just need to follow Him.

When I pastored in Alabama, I received a letter from a small church on the southside of Birmingham. They were down to just thirteen people in attendance and were considering closing their doors. Their pastor wanted to get them to turn their focus outward. In a desperate move, he said one Sunday, "Let's take our whole offering today and give it to another church and see what happens."

They knew from watching television that our church in Gardendale was in a building program. So they sent us their entire offering from that morning, $662. When I opened their letter and saw that check, I knew I was looking at the widow's mite. I read the letter to our deacons and said, "Do you think the Lord would have us reciprocate and take up an offering for them?"

We agreed to do so during our Stewardship Month that next January. We told our congregation about the offering they'd sent us and then said, "Today, we're going to take up an offering to give back to them!" We passed the offering plates, and the total was just under $29,000. We gave that money to that struggling congregation, and we were *both* blessed. They gave much of it to missions, paved their parking lot, and used the rest for outreach. And their church started to grow again! Our needs continued to be met, even without that $29,000. It's wonderful when we focus on an audience of One. The Lord led them and He also led us.

No Other Name

I try to say the name *Jesus* as often as possible. I recognize that *God, Lord,* and *Christ* are all good, biblical terms. But there's something special about the name *Jesus*. *Jesus* literally means "Jehovah is salvation." Peter told a hostile panel of religious leaders, "There is salvation in no one else, for there is no other name under heaven given to people by which we must be saved" (Acts 4:12). The people he addressed that day weren't thrilled to hear it, just as some aren't happy hearing His name today. But their displeasure doesn't change the fact of the unique power of Jesus Christ.

Charles Haddon Spurgeon once told some young preachers in training:

> Let your sermons be full of Christ, from begin-
> ning to end crammed full of the Gospel. As

for myself, brethren, I cannot preach anything else but Christ and His cross, for I know nothing else, and long ago, like the apostle Paul, I determined not to know anything else save Jesus Christ and Him crucified. . . . Preach Jesus Christ, brethren, always and everywhere; and every time you preach be sure to have much of Jesus Christ in your sermon. . . . We preach Jesus Christ to those who want Him, and we also preach Him to those who do not want Him, and we keep on preaching Christ until we make them feel that they do want Him, and cannot do without Him.[6]

No wonder thousands attended London's Metropolitan Tabernacle every Sunday to hear Spurgeon preach! People on the third level of the Tabernacle had to stand throughout the service. Thousands were saved, orphanages were begun, and a Bible college as well. Dignitaries from Parliament came and sat alongside the poor and illiterate. The Communists purportedly said that one reason their movement failed to take hold in England was because Spurgeon reached the poor people before they could impact them with their teachings of socialism.

When this "Prince of Preachers" died in 1892, an estimated 350,000 people lined the streets of London to watch his horse-drawn cortege pass by. All because a preacher and a church lifted high the name of Jesus.

The apostle Paul wrote, "For me, to live is Christ" (Phil. 1:21). Might we also extend his thought in this vein: *To worship is Christ. To do church is Christ.* It all revolves around the audience of One.

A preacher has failed miserably if the people who attend a worship service he leads listen to his sermon and leave saying to one another, "What a sermon!" "What a church!" "What a preacher!" However, if they leave saying, "What a Savior!" the preacher has triumphed! We must point the people to the only One worthy—Jesus.

It will be a watershed day when your church realizes that Jesus is the only One in "the audience" during a worship service. The rest of us are to be worshippers. We aren't ticket holders attending a performance. We are participants actively worshipping Him. *That* is biblical worship!

When we offer our worship and praise, our audience must be Jesus and Jesus alone!

Chapter 4

WELCOMING GOD'S GLORY

The Old Testament highlights many accounts of the Lord manifesting His glory to His people. That's remarkable considering Israel's perpetual sinful acts of idolatry and immorality. Yet, whenever the Israelites repented and returned to the Lord, He graciously forgave them. He revived them by repairing their spiritual brokenness and renewing their fervor for Him.

In the Old Testament, three Hebrew words refer to "revival." The first is *chayah*. It means "to live" or "to make alive." We see it in Psalm 85:6: "Will you not *revive* us again so that your people may rejoice in you?" (emphasis added). The second Hebrew word is *chadash*. It means to "repair" or "renew." King David prayed in Psalm 51:10: "God, create a clean heart for me and *renew* a steadfast spirit within me" (emphasis added). The final word is *chalap*, which means "to renew." It appears in Isaiah 40:31: "But those who trust in the LORD will *renew* their strength; they will soar on wings like eagles; they will run and not become weary, they will walk and not faint" (emphasis added).

When God's people repented, the Lord "made alive, repaired, and renewed" in awesome displays of His glory.

Corporate Visitations of God's Glory

When God revealed Himself to guide and protect His people, He prospered them and routed their enemies. Let's look at some Old Testament examples of God's glory filling His house and altering Israel's history.

God's Glory with God's People under Moses

The people of Israel went to Egypt during the days of Joseph, his eleven brothers, and their aged father, Jacob. After that generation died, the Israelites became slaves to the Egyptians. After four hundred years, God called Moses to lead His people out of slavery and into the promised land of Canaan. The Lord sent ten plagues that routed the Egyptians. Then God parted the Red Sea, and the Israelites passed through on dry land. When the Egyptian army followed, God closed the waters and destroyed them.

After that, Moses received the Ten Commandments at Mount Sinai. The Bible says, "When Moses went up the mountain, the cloud covered it. The glory of the LORD settled on Mount Sinai, and the cloud covered it for six days. On the seventh day he called to Moses from the cloud. The appearance of the LORD's glory to the Israelites was like a consuming fire on the mountaintop" (Exod. 24:15–17). Indeed, God displayed His glory on Mount Sinai.

But at the same time, the Israelites rebelled against the Lord by engaging in idolatry and immorality. When Moses finally descended from the mountain and saw Israel's sin, he threw the stone tablets with the Ten Commandments and shattered them on the ground. The Levites then killed three thousand of the Israelites who had instigated the idolatry. Moses ground the calf idol they had worshipped into powder, mixed it in water, and forced the Israelites to drink it (cf. Exod. 32).

After all that, the Lord refused to go with Israel into the promised land. But when the people repented and Moses interceded, the Lord forgave them. They built the tabernacle where the Israelites met with God. The Bible says, "So Moses finished the work. The cloud covered the tent of meeting, and the glory of the LORD filled the tabernacle. Moses was unable to enter the tent of meeting because the cloud rested on it, and the glory of the LORD filled the tabernacle" (Exod. 40:33–35). God's glory once again dwelt among His people!

God's Glory with God's People under Elijah

Elijah lived during troublesome times. After King Solomon's death, Israel divided. Israel's northern ten tribes rebelliously pulled away from Judah and Benjamin and erected two calf idols to worship, one in Dan and the other in Bethel. They ordered God's people to stop worshipping in Jerusalem. Ahab, the king of Israel at that time, was corrupt. He and his wicked wife, Jezebel, killed many of the Lord's prophets. They also led Israel to worship Baal, a pagan fertility idol.

God responded by sending a drought that lasted three years. In that setting, Elijah challenged Ahab and his prophets of Baal to a spiritual showdown on top of Mount Carmel. The pagans would pray to Baal, and Elijah would pray to the Lord. The God who sent fire from heaven upon the sacrifices would be pronounced as the true God.

Elijah confronted the unbelieving Israelites and said, "'How long will you waver between two opinions? If the LORD is God, follow him. But if Baal, follow him.' But the people didn't answer him a word" (1 Kings 18:21).

Baal's prophets offered their sacrifices first. They prayed, shouted, and danced for hours in a frenzied effort to gain Baal's attention. "But there was no sound; no one answered, no one paid attention" (1 Kings 18:29).

Elijah began to mock them all, and then he called God's people together. He repaired Jehovah's altar, and then had the altar soaked with water so everyone would know the fire was from God, not man. After that, Elijah prayed, "LORD, the God of Abraham, Isaac, and Israel, today let it be known that you are God in Israel and I am your servant, and that at your word I have done all these things. Answer me, LORD! Answer me so that this people will know that you, the LORD, are God and that you have turned their hearts back" (1 Kings 18:36–37).

God's fire fell from heaven and consumed the offering, the altar, and the water around the altar (cf. 1 Kings 18:38–39). God showed up in glory and showed off!

God's Glory with God's People under Solomon

After Israel was established in their new homeland, King David sought a permanent temple in Jerusalem. The Lord refused to allow David to build it because he had killed so many people in war. Consequently, Solomon, David's son, built the temple.

When Solomon completed the temple and the ark of the covenant was placed in the holy of holies, God's glory descended. "The temple, the LORD's temple, was filled with a cloud. And because of the cloud, the priests were not able to continue ministering, for *the glory of the LORD filled God's temple* (2 Chron. 5:13–14, emphasis added).

The same thing happened again when Solomon dedicated the temple to the Lord. "When Solomon finished praying, fire descended from heaven and consumed the burnt offering and the sacrifices, and *the glory of the LORD filled the temple.* The priests were not able to enter the LORD's temple because *the glory of the LORD filled the temple of the LORD.* All the Israelites were watching when the fire descended and *the glory of the LORD came on the temple.* They bowed down on the pavement with their faces to the ground. They worshiped and praised the LORD: 'For he is good, for his faithful love endures forever'" (2 Chron. 7:1–3, emphasis added).

"The glory of the Lord filled the temple of the Lord!" From that time forward, Israel associated the temple with the glory of God!

Personal Visitations of God's Glory

Wherever God touches down on earth, that site becomes sanctified. The Lord's presence makes it holy. Let's consider encounters with three individuals who experienced God's glory in the Old Testament.

Jacob's Personal Encounter with God's Glory

Jacob, the son of Isaac and grandson of Abraham, was a deceiver. He defrauded his brother Esau of his birthright and blessing that were due Esau as the elder son. Consequently, Jacob inherited the largest portion of Isaac's enormous estate. Isaac was rich because he was the sole heir of his father, Abraham, who was also wealthy (cf. Gen. 13:2). Isaac also farmed and had a hundredfold harvest in a single year (cf. Gen. 26:12).

When Jacob heard that Esau was about to murder him, he fled to Paddan-aram and lived there with his uncle Laban. En route to Laban, Jacob had a dream in which the Lord promised to bless, protect, and prosper him in Paddan-aram. He also promised Jacob that He'd bring him back to the promised land and bequeath it to Jacob's descendants! Jacob named that place Bethel, which meant "house of God." That was Jacob's first encounter with God's glory.

Jacob went on to serve his corrupt uncle Laban for twenty years. God used Laban to give Jacob a taste of the deception he'd inflicted upon Esau. When Jacob finally left Paddan-aram to return to the promised land, his angry brother Esau gathered four hundred men to kill him. At that critical moment, Jacob wrestled with a Man that was actually the angel of the Lord (Gen. 32). That Man dislocated Jacob's hip and "broke" Jacob like a trainer "breaks" a wild horse.

The Man then changed Jacob's name to "Israel," which means "he who struggles with God." That "Man" was the pre-incarnate "God-Man," Jesus Christ. Jacob wrestled with Jesus, Jesus won, and Jacob was blessed! From then on, Jacob walked with a holy limp and died still requiring a crutch (cf. Heb. 11:21).

When Esau arrived, he and Jacob reconciled. The Bible says, "Jacob then named the place Peniel, 'For I have seen God face to face,' he said, 'yet my life has been spared'" (Gen. 32:30). God revealed His glory to Jacob and turned his problems into blessings.

Moses's Personal Encounter with God's Glory

Moses was born a Hebrew slave. He was rescued from death as a baby and reared in the house of Pharaoh, the king of Egypt. Moses murdered an Egyptian taskmaster who mistreated a Hebrew slave. When Pharaoh heard about it, he tried to kill Moses. But Moses fled to Midian. There he married and became a shepherd. Forty years later, at the age of eighty, Moses saw a bush that was on fire, but it wasn't consumed. "When the LORD saw that he had gone over to look, God called out to him from the bush, 'Moses, Moses!' 'Here I am,' he answered. 'Do not come closer,' He said. 'Remove the sandals from your feet, for the place where you are standing is holy ground'" (Exod. 3:4–5). Through that burning bush and God's voice, Moses caught a glimpse of God's glory.

Later in life, Moses prayed to the Lord, "Please, let me see your glory" (Exod. 33:18). He had tasted God's glory at the burning bush and also on Mount Sinai. Yet Moses wanted more! That's the way it works. The more of God's glory you experience, the more you desire!

Moses asked God to allow him to see His face. Instead, the Lord said He would pass by Moses so he could see His back (cf. Exod. 33:19–23). On Mount Sinai, when Moses received the second copy of the Ten Commandments, the Lord passed by Moses and proclaimed His name. Moses saw the glory of God's back and worshiped Him (cf. Exod. 34:5–8). When Moses returned and met Aaron and the Israelites, his face reflected the glory of God. Moses covered his face with a veil, but whenever he appeared before the Lord, he removed it to bask in God's glory.

Isaiah's Personal Encounter with God's Glory

The prophet Isaiah lived in Judah under King Uzziah who reigned for fifty years. When Uzziah died, the nation mourned. That was when Isaiah saw the Lord. Although Judah's throne was empty, heaven's throne was occupied! Isaiah saw the angels worshipping the Lord and crying out antiphonally, "Holy, holy, holy is the LORD of Armies; his glory fills the whole earth" (Isa. 6:3). Isaiah fell flat in repentance, confessing his sin and the sins of his people. God cleansed Isaiah and called him to be His prophet. Isaiah said, "Here I am. Send me" (Isa. 6:8). God's manifest presence reveals sin, leads us to repentance, and helps us respond to God's call.

42

Over the years, God revealed His glory to Isaiah by giving him more messianic prophecies than any other Old Testament prophet. Isaiah prophesied about Jesus's virginal birth (Isa. 7:14), Jesus's deity (Isa. 9:6), and Jesus's death and resurrection (Isa. 53:1–12). Isaiah understood that the Messiah (Jesus) was to be God's ultimate revelation of His glory.

Conclusion

We see in the lives of Jacob, Moses, Solomon, Elijah, and Isaiah that God still desires for His people to long for His glory. When we repent and seek the Lord, He blesses us with His manifest presence. Some Christians, churches, and denominations today have "Ichabod" (i.e., "no glory") stamped on them. The only way we can reverse that is to welcome God's glory back into His churches and into our individual lives. Moses's desperate prayer should become the cry of all our hearts: *"Lord, show me Your glory!"*

Chapter 5

A CHURCH WITH LITTLE BUT GOD

Years ago I watched a movie titled *Glory Road*. It's based on the true story of the Texas Western University Miners, a men's college basketball team that had a great season in 1965–66. They upset the favored Kentucky Wildcats and won the 1966 NCAA national championship.

The David versus Goliath storyline in *Glory Road* focuses on the Miners' head coach, Don Haskins. Before coming to Texas Western, Haskins had no college-level coaching experience. But he was a man ahead of his time. Rather than recruiting locally, he selected players from some of the largest cities across the United States. He assembled a team loaded with talent. Most of his best players were African Americans, which wasn't the norm in the 1960s. Haskins and his players overcame racial differences and enjoyed a Cinderella season. Early on, few people believed in them, and hardly anyone gave them a chance in the national championship game against Kentucky, then coached by the legendary Adolph Rupp. Yet, against all odds, they defeated Rupp's Wildcats!

That little Texas team reminds me of the first-century Christians. They too were a hodgepodge of regular people—fishermen, tax collectors, political zealots, and others. Paul said that most of them were not wise, mighty, or noble. Instead, God had chosen the foolish, weak, and base people so no man could boast before Him (cf. 1 Cor. 1:26–29).

Yet, in spite of their lack of worldly accomplishments, they became brave soldiers of Christ. Even their enemies admitted they had "turned the world upside down" (Acts 17:6). They had little but God, yet they changed the world!

Today, we have Christian schools, bookstores, the Internet, media ministries, websites, staff members, elaborate facilities, and abundant wealth. But where is the power we see in the book of Acts? Let's look at the early church and see what God did, and what He can still do, when we place our "little" into His omnipotent hands.

A Praying Church

The only thing Jesus's disciples ever asked Him to teach them to do was to pray (cf. Luke 11:1). He did so by personally modeling prayer for them through His own prayers and also by giving them the Lord's Prayer as the pattern for calling on the Lord. As a result, the early Christians engaged in praise, thanksgiving, confession, petition, intercession, and spiritual warfare, both individually and corporately.

Before Jesus ascended to heaven, He commissioned His followers to take the gospel to the entire world (cf. Matt. 28:18–20; Acts 1:8). His command exceeded their human abilities. They needed the help of the Holy Spirit. After Jesus ascended to heaven, His followers "went to the room upstairs where they were staying. . . . They all were continually united in prayer" (Acts 1:13–14). The early church was birthed in a *united*, *protracted*, and *focused* prayer meeting.

No wonder God blessed Peter's sermon on Pentecost. God's people prayed ten days. They were filled with the Holy Spirit and witnessed to the lost. Peter preached a sermon that probably lasted less than an hour, and *3,000 people were saved*! Today, we reverse that. We pray less than an hour, preach for ten days, and see relatively few respond. It isn't God's fault or the gospel's fault. The fault is our own. We don't "pray the price."

A Witnessing Church

The early believers talked *to* God, but they also talked *about* God. They told everybody about Jesus everywhere they went. Each believer shared the gospel with lost people with the intent of leading them to repent of their sins, believe savingly in Jesus, and receive Him as Lord and Savior.

Witnessing to lost people was one of the primary reasons Jesus gave the Holy Spirit to Christians. Jesus said, "But you will receive power when the Holy Spirit has come upon you, *and you will be my witnesses*" (Acts 1:8, emphasis added). Philip, a layman and a deacon, was also a soul-winner in the early church (cf. Acts 6:1–7). In Samaria, he preached, cast out demons and healed the sick. Consequently, "there was great joy in that city" (Acts 8:8).

Later on, God told Philip to travel on a desert road that led to Gaza. He met a court official of the queen of Ethiopia who'd been to Jerusalem to worship the God of the Jews. Returning to Ethiopia, he was reading from Isaiah about the Messiah. When Philip overheard him reading, he "proceeded to tell him the good news about Jesus, beginning with that Scripture" (Acts 8:35). His witness was verbal, scriptural and Christ-centered. The man heard the gospel, repented of his sins, believed in Christ, and was saved and baptized. A soul-winning deacon led the first Gentile to Christ!

Philip reminds me of my late father-in-law, Dempsey Dodds. Like Philip, Mr. Dodds was a soul-winning deacon. After Mr. Dodds's seventieth birthday, he was trained in Evangelism Explosion, a curriculum for training Christians to become personal soul-winners. When he died at the age of ninety-one, we found a little book in which he had inscribed the names of hundreds of people he had personally led to faith in Christ. Being the humble man he was, he never told anyone about that book or those names. I believe each name is also written in the Lamb's Book of Life in heaven. That's the kind of witnessing you see in Acts: Christians opening their mouths, sharing Jesus from the Scriptures and people being saved.

My friend, Pastor James Merritt, frequently asks two questions to Christians: 1) "When was the last time you led someone to faith in Christ?" 2) "When was the last time you tried?" Those are great questions to ponder. If you want to be like the early Christians, be Christ's witness.

A Miraculous Church

The early church was miraculous. It could only be explained by acknowledging that God was in their midst. Does anything ever happen at your church that is unexplainable apart from God's power? What took place in the churches in Acts couldn't be described by human persuasiveness, power, or personality. It was truly "a God thing."

After 3,000 people were saved on the day of Pentecost, "everyone was filled with awe, and many wonders and signs were being performed through the apostles" (Acts 2:43). Can that be said about your church? Are lost people being saved? Are sick people being healed? Are people being set free from sinful strongholds such as alcoholism, drug abuse, homosexuality, or pornography? Are broken families being restored and put back together?

Since miracles occurred among the earliest Christians, shouldn't they occur at least once in a while in our churches today? Some object and say, "The day of miracles has passed." Friend, there has never been a *day* of miracles, but there is and always will be a *God* of miracles. Jesus does warn us that "an evil and adulterous generation demands a sign" (Matt. 16:4) But nowhere does Scripture say that miracles can't occur today. If we follow Jesus, signs and wonders should at least occasionally follow us. Believers in Jesus should do His works (cf. John 14:12).

A church with little but God will at times be characterized by miracles. God will "do above and beyond all that we ask or think according to the power that works in us" (Eph. 3:20). It will be a church known for the miraculous presence and power of God.

A Spirit-Led Church

The early Christians were filled with and led by the Holy Spirit. When the Spirit came at Pentecost, He indwelt every believer. From then on, they began to listen to His still, small voice and obey His promptings.

In Acts 16, Paul and his companions were on a mission trip. They needed to decide where they should go next to preach the gospel. On two different occasions, they started to go into specific regions, but each time God's Spirit said no (cf. Acts 16:6–7). *They* wanted to go one way, but *the Spirit* said no! The Spirit knew that Paul and his fellow missionaries would be more effective in Macedonia. Wisely, they followed His guidance.

Does God's Spirit lead your church like that? Many churches have a similar testimony of John the Baptist's disciples in Ephesus. When asked if they had received the Spirit, they replied, "We haven't even heard that there is a Holy Spirit" (Acts 19:2). Sound familiar?

Some might object and say, "God gives us a mind to think. Just use common sense!" Did common sense cause Noah to build his ark or lead Abraham to be willing to offer up his son, Isaac, as a burnt offering? Did common sense prompt Paul and Silas to sing praises to God after they were beaten and imprisoned at Philippi? The Spirit won't always lead you according to common sense. Scripture says, "Trust in the LORD with all your heart, and *do not rely on your own understanding*" (Prov. 3:5).

God's ways and thoughts won't always be the same as man's thoughts, but they will always be *superior* to man's (cf. Isa. 55:8–9). If God's Spirit is leading you to do or say something, you should obey, even when you don't understand. Failure to do so will quench the Spirit's power in your life. Those who are *led by the Spirit* are children of God (cf. Rom. 8:14).

A Growing Church

The church with little but God grew exponentially. On the day of Pentecost, they expanded from 120 praying people (Acts 1:15) to more than 3,000 (Acts 2:41) born-again believers! And they continued to grow numerically. The Bible says, "Every day the Lord added to their number those who were being saved" (Acts 2:47). They grew by means of conversion. There weren't any other churches from which members could transfer. People were saved and the church flourished.

Church growth was actually a by-product, not a goal, of the early church. Worshipping and sharing Jesus were their priorities. Church growth was the natural result. Jesus said *He* would build His church (Matt. 16:18). Those early Christians humbly lived holy lives, loved lost people and one another, and shared the gospel in the power of the Spirit. They planted and watered gospel seed, and *God* miraculously caused the growth!

Some people today don't believe churches should be large. Yet the church in the book of Acts was *very* large. The number of believers in Jerusalem grew to five thousand men, not including the women and children (cf. Acts 4:4)! They counted people because people matter to God!

One of my favorite verses in Acts says, "So the church throughout all Judea, Galilee, and Samaria had peace and was strengthened. Living in the fear of the Lord and encouraged by the Holy Spirit, *it increased in numbers*" (Acts 9:31, emphasis added). They had unity, spiritual growth, edification, and reverent worship, and they also experienced remarkable numerical growth!

I've heard people say, "Large churches are not as friendly as small churches." Do you really think churches grow to be large because they aren't friendly? Others might say, "A church can get too big." Statements like that often come from a place of insecurity, where some might even feel threatened that they will lose their position of influence and be replaced by some "newcomer."

A church has room to grow as long as there are lost people who need to be saved. We care about the spiritual health of a church because we want it to grow. The church with little but God understands that and keeps growing. Look at the church in the book of Acts and then look at our churches today and ask, "Why are we so different from them?"

When Elijah went to heaven, his successor, Elisha, asked in anguish, "Where is the LORD God of Elijah?" (2 Kings 2:14). (I.e., "Where is the God who performed great and mighty miracles in our midst?")

Like Elisha, I sometimes feel like shouting, "Where is the God of the book of Acts?" The early church had little but God, and their amazing growth proved that He was more than enough.

In the next two chapters, I invite you to walk with me through some short histories of revival to see what we can glean from those experiences. After that, we'll consider some essential components of a church prepared for revival.

Chapter 6

AMERICAN REVIVALS IN THE EIGHTEENTH AND NINETEENTH CENTURIES

I t is impossible to understand America's history without appreciating the great spiritual awakenings that molded this country in previous years. Those revivals breathed new life into denominations, churches, and individual Christians. Churches were strengthened, new churches were established, and social advances were made in schools, orphanages, and hospitals. Let's examine the revivals in America during the 1700s and 1800s.

The First Great Awakening

In the mid-1700s, God moved mightily in the American colonies. Bushman said it was "like the civil rights demonstrations, the campus disturbances, and the urban riots of the 1960s combined . . . in their impact on national life."[7]

America's population grew exponentially in the early 1700s. In one century, the thirteen American colonies grew to more than half a million people. They came primarily from Europe, while slave trade also populated the southern colonies.

Wars on the colonies' western frontiers led to a spirit of fear among many of the settlers. Drunkenness, sexual immorality, and lack of respect for human life were societal norms that caused churches to struggle. In 1662, Puritans established "The Half-Way Covenant," allowing people who had merely been baptized, but not necessarily converted to Christ, to join a church. Consequently, congregations took in many unconverted members. Into that setting, God called some godly preachers to lead in a revival.

In 1720, a young preacher from the Netherlands named **Theodore J. Frelinghuysen (1691–1747)** arrived in New York. He longed to see revival in the Dutch Reformed Church. George Whitefield, called Frelinghuysen "the beginner of the great work"[8] (i.e., the First Great Awakening). Frelinghuysen stressed that only those who had been converted should consider themselves to be Christians. Baptism and church membership were not enough. He also stressed that Christians should live holy lives. As he ministered in New Jersey, revival broke out. The Dutch Reformed Church eventually split into pro-revival and anti-revival groups. Those who favored revival founded Queens College, which eventually became Rutgers University.

William Tennent Sr. (1673–1746), a Presbyterian minister, built a log cabin to train his sons in theology. Soon, similar log colleges emerged across the colonies. They were precursors to modern seminaries. Tennent's log cabin eventually evolved into Princeton University. Tennent's son, **Gilbert Tennent (1703–1764)**, helped spread the Awakening. In 1740, he preached a scathing sermon entitled "The Danger of an Unconverted Ministry." He said most of the Presbyterian clergy of his day were not true Christians. "Is a blind man fit to be a guide? Is a dead man fit to bring others to life? Is a mad man fit to give counsel in matters of life and death? . . . Isn't an unconverted minister like a man who would learn (i.e., teach) others to swim, before he has learned it himself, and so is drowned in the act, and dies like a fool?"[9] Tennent infuriated many, but the Lord used him to bring awakening.

The greatest theologian of the First Great Awakening was **Jonathan Edwards (1703–1758)**. Edwards graduated from Yale as valedictorian of his class when he was only seventeen. In 1792, he succeeded his grandfather, Solomon Stoddard, as pastor of the Congregational church in Northampton, Massachusetts. The congregation grew, and revival began to spread in and around Northampton.

Edward's most famous sermon, "Sinners in the Hands of an Angry God," was based on Deuteronomy 32:35 (KJV), "Their foot shall slide in due time." When he first preached that sermon in Enfield, Connecticut, on July 8, 1741, Edwards boldly declared that the only thing that prevents anyone from going to hell is God's pleasure. Man is like a spider hanging helplessly over a flame, held back from destruction by a thin cord of God's making. Gunther describes the audience's response to his sermon,

[His sermon] was interrupted by outcries from
the congregation—men and women stood up
and rolled on the floor, their cries once drown-
ing out the voice of the preacher. Some are
said to have laid on the pillars and braces of
the church, apparently feeling that at that very
moment their feet were sliding, that they were
being precipitated into hell. All through the
house one could hear the cries of those feeling themselves lost, crying to God for mercy.
Through the night Enfield was like a belea-
guered city. In almost every house men and
women could be heard crying out for God to
save them.[10]

Some ridiculed the Awakening as religious fanaticism.
Dallimore says, "Throughout New England . . . two antagonistic
bodies began to form, the one favoring it and the other oppos-
ing it. These were later to be termed the *New Lights* and the
Old Lights."[11] The Awakening's leading opponent was Charles
Chauncy (1705–1787). He opposed all religious enthusiasm of
his day. His liberal theology paved the way for the Unitarian
movement, which later engulfed many American churches in its
heretical beliefs.

Eventually, Edwards's congregation grew weary of his strict-
ness and forced him to resign. He left and went to Stockbridge,
where he ministered among Native Americans until 1757 when
he was elected president of Princeton University. But he soon

contracted smallpox and died in 1758. Edwards's brilliant theological writings are still influential today.

One of the first revival "celebrities" in America was a young English preacher named **George Whitefield (1714–1770)**. Whitefield "may have been the best-known Protestant in the whole world during the eighteenth century. . . . He was the single best-known religious leader in America of that century, and the most widely recognized figure of any sort in North America before George Washington."[12] While Edwards was the greatest theologian of the First Great Awakening, Whitefield was its greatest preacher. Over thirty-four years, Whitefield preached 18,000 times, primarily outdoors. He often attracted crowds of ten to twenty thousand. His extemporaneous style and melodious voice kept listeners spellbound. He influenced men such as Benjamin Franklin. Although Franklin never retracted his Deism, he supported Whitefield financially and published many of his sermons. Whitefield's itinerant ministry connected multiple pockets of revival into one gigantic spiritual awakening. He preached the night before he died in Newburyport, Massachusetts, where he was buried under the pulpit of the local Presbyterian church.

In the southern colonies of the 1700s, the primary Christian denominations were Baptist, Presbyterian, and Methodist. Two of the leading Baptists of the colonial era were **Isaac Backus (1724–1806)** and **Shubal Stearns (1706–1771)**. Backus began as a Congregationalist but came to believe that immersion was the biblical mode of baptism. He was therefore baptized through immersion following conversion and became a Baptist pastor in

1756. He served the same church in Connecticut for fifty years. He also traveled extensively by horseback preaching thousands of evangelistic sermons. Shubal Stearns was another Baptist preacher God used mightily in the Awakening. He was saved listening to George Whitefield preach. Stearns helped spread revival in the Carolinas and Virginia.

The Second Great Awakening

In time, the First Great Awakening lost momentum. But at the end of the 1700s and the early 1800s, the Lord sent the Second Great Awakening. Noll says it was more important than the First Awakening: "The Second Great Awakening was the most influential revival of Christianity in the history of the United States."[13]

Immediately after the First Awakening came the Revolutionary War (1775–1783). Prior to the war, most people in the colonies were religious. Yet when multiple American preachers left their churches to fight the British, those leaderless churches began to decline. As a result, drunkenness, profanity, gambling, robbery, and sexual promiscuity became rampant across the nation.

The French Enlightenment also fueled spiritual decadence. Opponents of Christianity such as Hume, Rousseau, and Voltaire ushered in anti-Christian philosophies such as Deism, skepticism, and atheism. Even colonial war heroes such as Thomas Paine and Ethan Allen joined the attack against Christianity in America. Many American colleges became seedbeds of liberalism.

Ironically, the Lord sent spiritual awakening to several college campuses. The Second Great Awakening probably began at **Hampden-Sydney College** in Virginia. Toward the end of the 1780s, most of the students at Hampden-Sydney were, like their counterparts across the nation, cynical of religion. Yet four sincere Christian students—William Hull, Cary Allen, James Blythe, and Clement Reid—decided to meet for prayer, Bible study, and theological discussions. When the other students found out about their gatherings, the campus nearly experienced a riot.

Providentially, the president of the college, John Blair Smith, who had been converted to Christ during the First Great Awakening, stopped the persecution against Christian students and began to meet with them. Others soon joined. As they prayed, studied Scripture, and discussed theology, revival occurred. "Soon half of the students were deeply impressed and under conviction, and the revival spread rapidly through the neighborhood."[14]

Revival also touched down at **Yale University** under the leadership of **Timothy Dwight (1752–1817)**, grandson of Jonathan Edwards. When Dwight became president of Yale in 1795, he confronted opponents of Christianity. Through his character, preaching, and apologetic reasoning, students began listening to Dwight, and many were converted. "The salvation of the soul was the great subject of thought, of conversation, of absorbing interest; the convictions of many were pungent and overwhelming; and the 'peace of believing' which succeeded, was not less strongly marked."[15] By 1802, Yale experienced awakening. "A third of the 225 students were converted, and many of these became agents for revival and reform in New England, upstate New York, and the West."[16]

At **Williams College** in Massachusetts, revival broke out among students, including Samuel Mills. In 1806, as students gathered for prayer, a rainstorm drove them to seek shelter at a haystack. It was there that Mills was called to become a missionary. Two years later, he and others requested that the General Association of Massachusetts send them to minister in India. On June 28, 1810, the association founded the first foreign mission board in America, the American Board of Commissioners for Foreign Missions. By 1812, Adoniram Judson, Samuel Nott, Luther Rice, Gordon Hall, and Samuel Newell were commissioned as missionaries at the Tabernacle Congregational Church in Salem, Massachusetts. Mills never went to India, selflessly giving up his spot to Gordon Hall who was the better linguist of the two.

The Second Great Awakening also spread by means of **Frontier Camp Meetings**. In 1797, Presbyterian pastor James McGready led his church in Logan County, Kentucky, to pray every Saturday evening, Sunday morning, and the third Saturday of each month for a year. They prayed for awakening in their county and around the world. When McGready instigated the first "camp" meeting," people came from miles around. They prayed, sang, listened to preaching and repented of sin. **Barton Stone (1772–1844)** visited McGready's camp meeting and was moved deeply. Stone went back and held a similar camp meeting at Cane Ridge, Kentucky, in 1801. More than twenty thousand

Presbyterian, Baptist, and Methodist pastors and parishioners gathered at Cane Ridge. Many lost people were converted to Christ, and many Christians experienced a deep renewal and zeal for spiritual matters. Multiple churches were also birthed out of that movement.

The renewed interest of the faith touched off at Cane Ridge and similar camp meetings led to a rapid growth of Presbyterian churches in the South. By comparison, however, Presbyterian efforts paled beside the accomplishments of the Methodists and Baptists. Methodist circuit riders and Baptist farmer-preachers fanned out through the South and the open West in unprecedented numbers. By the 1830s these groups had replaced the Congregationalists and Presbyterians as the largest denominations not only in the South but in the whole United States.[17]

The Cane Ridge meeting led to many other successful camp meetings.

Itinerant Methodist preachers known as circuit riders also helped spread revival across the American frontiers. They took the gospel to isolated areas of population in the East. The most famous circuit rider was Methodist patriarch, **Frances Asbury (1745–1816)**. In 1772, John Wesley, leader of the Methodists in England, appointed Asbury as leader of American Methodism. Over the years, Asbury rode on horseback approximately 300,000 miles and preached 16,500 times. During the Revolutionary War, he refused to return to England saying, "I can by no means agree to leave such a field for gathering souls to Christ, as we have in America. It would be an eternal dishonor to the Methodists, that we should all leave three thousand souls, who desire to commit themselves to our care; neither is it the part of a good shepherd to leave his flock in time of danger; therefore, I am determined, by the grace of God, not to leave them, let the consequence be what it may."[18] When the war ended, Asbury was still alive and preaching.

Asbury favored the camp meetings. In a letter, he described the Cane Ridge Camp Meeting, saying, "The work of God is running like fire in Kentucky. It is reported that near fifteen if not twenty thousand were present at one Sacramental occasion of the Presbyterians; and one thousand if not fifteen hundred . . . felt the power of grace."[19]

Asbury was very disciplined. He rose by 5:00 a.m. and retired by 9:00 p.m. He studied his Bible and read other books as he rode his horse, covering up to a hundred pages per day. One journal entry says that on one occasion he read through the entire Bible in only four months. Asbury became the symbol of American Methodism.

Another famous Methodist circuit-riding preacher was **Peter Cartwright (1785–1872)**. He too supported the camp meetings and road across western America, preaching more than 15,000 times. He would stay in a community until there was a response. He denounced slavery and liquor as he preached. He also ran for the U.S. Congress, losing to Abraham Lincoln.

The most important figure of the Second Great Awakening was **Charles Grandison Finney (1792–1875)**. Finney was a lawyer when he converted to Christ. He rejected theological training at Princeton. Instead, he used reasoning and logic, which he had learned as a lawyer. He argued the Lord's case from

Scripture. His preaching was passionate, polished, and persuasive. He turned from staunch Calvinism to preach a gospel of free salvation. He believed in a general atonement while at the same time maintaining the doctrine of election, insisting that man's free will and God's sovereignty were compatible concepts. He preached for a verdict offering people the opportunity to make decisions for Christ at the conclusion of his messages.

The most fruitful years of his ministry were from 1824 to 1832. He traveled countless miles, preaching numerous revival meetings. The greatest revival he preached was in Rochester, New York. Many were saved and more than forty men became preachers and missionaries.

Eventually, Finney's health failed due to his relentless schedule. He stopped traveling as much and became the pastor of the Broadway Tabernacle in New York City. During the fall of 1834 and winter of 1835, Finney gave twenty-two lectures on revival to his congregation. They were put into book form under the title *Lectures on Revivals of Religion*,[20] popularly known as *Revival Lectures*. In those lectures, Finney insisted that revival is not primarily a miracle sent from heaven. Rather, it is the result of the correct use of biblical methods. He stressed that just as a farmer plants seeds and bears a harvest, even so God sends revival when we appropriate the God-given means that produce it.

Finney popularized several "New Measures" in his evangelistic meetings. In the *anxious meeting*, people who were concerned about their spiritual condition were gathered so Finney could lead them to Christ. *Anxious seats* at the front of sanctuaries were reserved for people to sit down and be converted to Christ. Those seats were a precursor to public, evangelistic invitations. Finney's *protracted meeting* was a series of revival services held on consecutive nights, instead of weekends, which was previously the norm.

Until Finney, revival had been understood primarily as a sovereign work of God. He stressed that God would send revival if people would meet His prerequisites. That was a new concept, and it was difficult for hard-core Calvinists to embrace.

Finney's "New Measures" were especially opposed by a Calvinistic evangelist named **Asahel Nettleton (1783–1844)**. Nettleton was a student at Yale when revival broke out under Timothy Dwight. Nettleton traveled extensively for years as an itinerant preacher, often leading hundreds to faith in Christ in a single evangelistic service. While he and Finney disagreed concerning election, the Lord used both of them in revival, just as he had used both Wesley, an Armenian, and Whitefield, a Calvinist, in the 1700s.

The Prayer Revival of 1858

By the late 1850s, the Second Awakening was waning, and American churches were declining. "From 1843 to 1857, the additions to the churches scarcely equaled the losses sustained by death, removal or discipline, while a widespread indifference to religion became prevalent."[21]

The Gold Rush of 1849 demonstrated that many Americans were more interested in gold than God. In 1857, the nation's banking industry crashed, and numerous citizens lost everything.

The country was also bitterly divided over slavery. Southern states were making plans to break away from their northern neighbors and start a new nation.

In that setting, God chose laymen, not preachers, to spark a spiritual awakening. Across America, many godly laymen were concerned about the nation's declining spiritual state. Lay-led prayer meetings began forming simultaneously. Perhaps the most famous of these took place in New York City on Fulton Street in the financial district.

In 1857, the North Reformed Dutch Church in New York called a businessman named **Jeremiah Lanphier (1809–1898)** to serve as a lay minister. People were leaving the downtown district to move to neighboring residential areas. As Lanphier walked the streets of Manhattan, he noticed discouraged businessmen, spiritually decadent citizens, and apathetic churches. He offered a simple prayer: "Lord, what wilt Thou have *me* to do?"

He decided to host a prayer meeting for businessmen. They would meet once a week at noon for an hour at his church on Fulton Street and pray for spiritual awakening. The business-men could come and go to accommodate their busy schedules. Lanphier passed out fliers inviting men to attend. The first prayer meeting was held on September 23, 1857. Roy Fish described what happened that day: "For thirty minutes, Lanphier prayed alone. At 12:30, a step was heard on the stairs. Soon another came, and another, until finally six men were there to inaugurate the Fulton Street prayer meetings. It was almost prophetic of a proper spirit of cooperation that, at the first meeting, the six men present represented four different denominations."[22]

The next week, twenty men showed up to pray. The following week, between thirty and forty men came to pray. The format was simple: take requests, pray, share testimonies (no preaching, even!). They soon decided to pray daily instead of weekly. On October 14, more than one hundred men attended the meeting, many of them unconverted. The meetings grew, and before the close of the second month, all three of the lecture rooms of the church were filled. Within six months of the beginning date, as many as fifty thousand were attending this and other prayer meetings daily in New York alone. Within two years, the fires of revival had swept the entire nation, and some one million people had been added to the churches nationally.[23]

The nation's population at that time was 30 million. That means approximately one out of every thirty Americans encountered Christ, either by conversion or rededication!

The revival sent spiritual shock waves across America. In Chicago, a young shoe salesman named **Dwight Lyman Moody (1837–1899)** was saved and started a Sunday School class, which eventually became a church that bore his name. He also led people to Christ through Chicago's Young Men's Christian Association (YMCA).

With Moody's ministry, "business principles entered the field of mass evangelism."[24] He introduced large-scale preparation and organization for revival meetings. He traveled across America and to England preaching the gospel. He and his evangelistic musician, Ira D. Sankey, enjoyed success similar to Whitefield's ministry in the 1700s. His preaching was theologically conservative, understandable, and aimed at the common man. Like Jesus, common people heard D. L. Moody gladly.

Conclusion

Our nation was birthed in revival. Prior to the Revolutionary War, the First Great Awakening rekindled the spiritual fervor of the previous Puritans and Pilgrims. God used great preachers to usher in spiritual renewal among the people in the colonies.

A Second Awakening at the end of the 1700s lasted into the early 1800s. Gospel preachers traveled across the expanding nation and brought the gospel to masses of people, even to those in the remote regions of the west. Revival fires burned from urban college campuses to rural camp meetings.

Then, in the mid-1800s, God used laymen to pray and usher in another revival. Those prayer meetings ignited an awakening just before 600,000-plus souls from the North and South fell slain on America's soil during the Civil War. Revival would not occur in America again until the turn of the twentieth century.

Chapter 7

AMERICAN REVIVALS FROM
1900 TO THE PRESENT

S ince the early part of the twentieth century, there have been
three significant awakenings in America. At the dawn of the
1900s, revival swept across America and much of the world. Prior
to the next awakening in the 1950s, two world wars occurred,
with the Great Depression sandwiched in between. Then during
the 1960s, which were years of social upheaval in America, beginning in 1967, God sent a revival primarily among the youth.
That was the last spiritual awakening America has experienced
at a regional or national scale.

The Revival of 1904–1908

The Welsh Revival

In 1904, revival occurred in America as part of a worldwide
revival that began in Wales. In 1902, at a Keswick Convention
in England, a group of Christians formed a "circle of prayer for

world-wide revival,"[25] where many Welsh preachers were touched by God.

The Welsh Revival began with a pastor named **Joseph Jenkins (1859–1929)** from New Quay, Cardiganshire. In 1903, Jenkins began to seek the Lord for personal revival. He changed the formality of his church's worship services. Members began to share testimonies, pray, read Scripture, and sing as the Lord prompted. One Sunday, Jenkins asked his youth to share testimonies. A young girl named Florrie Evans said, "If no one else will, then I must say that I do love the Lord Jesus Christ with all my heart." With that statement, the Holy Spirit fell upon the meeting and started an amazing revival in New Quay.

After six months, a young pastor named Seth Joshua attended a meeting and was touched by God. A young man named **Evan Roberts (1878–1951)** heard Joshua preach. At one of the services, Joshua prayed, "Lord, bend us." Roberts knelt and prayed, "Lord, bend *me*."

Roberts soon became the focus of the revival. He believed God told him 100,000 people in Wales would come to Christ. In the fall of 1904, Roberts returned to his hometown of Lougher and preached his four tenets of revival: 1) Put away any unconfessed sin. 2) Put away any doubtful habit. 3) Obey the Spirit promptly. 4) Confess Christ publicly. Within six months more than 100,000 people were saved, just as he had envisioned. Wales was aglow with heavenly fire. People came from all over the world to experience the Lord's work. Revival spread to all of Great Britain, as well as across Europe, India, Africa, Latin America, the Orient, Australia, and North America.

Revival in the United States

In 1900, America needed spiritual awakening. As the population exploded and technological advancements emerged, America became a worldwide industrial powerhouse. Many Americans moved to the cities, abandoning their agricultural roots. Nine million immigrants came to America between 1900 and 1910. Many were Catholics who found themselves in a predominantly Protestant nation.

Several disturbing, theologically unorthodox trends emerged in America. **Mary Baker Eddy (1821–1910)** founded the Christian Science Church in 1879. In 1884, **Charles Taze Russell (1852–1916)** started the Jehovah's Witnesses. In addition to these cults, theological liberals such as **Washington Gladden (1836–1918)** and **Walter Rauschenbusch (1861–1918)** advanced the Social Gospel movement. They ministered to social problems without emphasizing man's need of salvation in Christ.

In that spiritually dismal setting, many American Christians began to pray. In 1905, several college and seminary campuses reported movements of God among students. From 1904 to 1908, traveling evangelists who followed D. L. Moody's example reached cities for Christ by means of area-wide crusades.

One of those evangelists was **Reuben Archer Torrey (1856–1928)**. He graduated from Yale in 1878. In 1889 he became the superintendent of the Chicago Evangelization Society and the Moody Bible Institute. From 1894 to 1905, Torrey served as pastor of the Chicago Avenue Baptist Church. From 1902, he held overseas evangelistic crusades and led multitudes to Christ in

Great Britain, Germany, India, New Zealand, Australia, China, and Japan.

John Wilbur Chapman (1859–1918) was a Presbyterian evangelist in the early 1900s. In 1878, he attended a revival meeting where D. L. Moody was preaching. Moody counseled Chapman personally using John 5:24 to give Chapman assurance of his salvation. Chapman became a pastor from 1885 to 1890 and led the First Reformed Church of Albany, New York. It grew from 150 to 1,500 in attendance. His wife died in 1886. Chapman remarried, and in 1890 he became pastor of the Bethany Presbyterian Church in Philadelphia, which had one of the largest Sunday schools in the world. More than 1,000 of his church members gathered weekly to pray for him. Many people were saved and the church grew. Chapman's final pastorate, the Fourth Presbyterian Church in New York, also experienced growth.

Chapman began his itinerant evangelistic ministry in 1904, conducting citywide meetings using highly structured organization. He took seventeen evangelists to Pittsburgh. Dividing the city into nine districts, they preached simultaneous crusades, and seven thousand people were saved. In 1907, another evangelist, Charles M. Alexander, joined him. In 1908, they went to Philadelphia with other evangelists. The combined attendance in the simultaneous crusades averaged 35,000 people for six weeks for a total attendance of 1,470,000, with 8,000 professing faith in Christ.

William "Billy" Ashley Sunday (1862–1935), a former professional baseball player, entered the ministry in 1891 working for the Chicago YMCA. In 1893, he served under J. Wilbur Chapman who taught him about organizing revival meetings. Sunday began preaching large evangelistic meetings and crusades. From the 1920s until his death in 1935, Sunday was well-known for his preaching, especially the antics and gestures he used as he addressed his audiences. He also strongly opposed the liquor industry.

During this time, the Lord spread revival through a Methodist preacher named **Sam Jones (1847–1906)**. Before his conversion, Jones was an alcoholic. In 1872, at his father's death-bed, in desperation he asked Christ to save him. Immediately he became a Methodist preacher, pastoring several churches until 1880 when he began to travel and preach. His itinerant ministry resulted in multitudes receiving Christ as Savior. In 1885, Jones preached in Nashville and led riverboat captain Tom Ryman to Christ. Ryman built the Union Gospel Tabernacle for Jones to use to evangelize that city. The tabernacle later became the Ryman Auditorium, the original home of the Grand Old Opry. To this day, the Ryman remains a historic concert venue in downtown Nashville, but it bears the architectural features of a church, complete with pews and stained-glass windows.

Rodney "Gypsy" Smith (1860–1947) was born in a tent and raised in a gypsy camp. He never went to school. He was converted to Christ in 1876. General William Booth asked him to work evangelistically in the Salvation Army where he served until 1882. He went on to preach all over the world, leading multitudes to faith in Jesus.

Azusa Street Revival

Charles Parham (1873–1929) was an evangelist. In 1900, he started a Bible school in Topeka, Kansas. There, Parham and several of his students began to speak in tongues. Parham left Kansas and moved to Houston, Texas, where he founded another school. One of his students was an African American preacher named **William J. Seymour (1870–1922)**. In 1906, Seymour left Houston to go to Los Angeles to become a pastor. He told his new congregation about his Pentecostal experience. They locked him out of the church, saying he was teaching heresy. Seymour joined another group of people that included Edward Lee. They too began to pray for the Pentecostal experience.

Crowds began to flock to the house on Bonnie Brae Street. Preachers preached from the front porch to the multitudes gathered on the street. In April 1906, the group moved to a former African Methodist Episcopal Church located at 312 Azusa Street which held about 350 people. By the fall, people were coming from all over. The Pentecostal movement that would eventually go worldwide had begun.

The Revival of the 1950s

The 1940s were bittersweet years in America. During the first half, America and its allies were engaged in World War II (WWII), fighting powerful enemies in Asia (Japan) and in Europe (Germany and Italy). WWII resulted in more than

400,000 deaths and hundreds of thousands of other soldiers being wounded.

When the war finally ended, millions of young American soldiers returned home to secure jobs and start careers and families. They sought a prosperous, happy lifestyle that became known as "the American dream." But all was not well. The Soviet Union, that had been a U.S. ally during the war, started forcing its doctrines of socialism on many European nations. Communism became the new global threat. The "cold war" resulted in a nuclear arms race between the two megapowers—Russia and the USA.

Following WWII, morality in America declined. While people were making more money than ever and the standard of living increased, so did alcoholism and divorce rates. Theological liberalism was rampant in many churches, colleges, and seminaries. The Social Gospel of the early 1900s was embraced by many. Conservative Christianity which emphasized biblical preaching, conversion, evangelism, and missions was quickly declining from many "mainline" denominations.

In April 1949, four young ministers—Billy Graham, J. Edwin Orr, William Dunlap, and Jack Frank—prayed in Graham's office in Minneapolis and asked God to send revival to college campuses in America. Orr went to Bethel, a Baptist college and seminary in Minneapolis, and lectured on revival. The school president, Henry Wingblade, canceled classes to allow students to participate in the prolonged chapel services. Dorm rooms were filled as students prayed and worshipped God, confessed their sins and made restitution with anyone they had wronged. A spirit of holiness pervaded the campus. Dr. Wingblade described the meetings by saying, "The Holy Spirit has wrought a marvelous work on our campus." Later, he said, "I do not think we have had anything quite like the wonderful meetings of last week in all the history of Bethel."[26]

Revival meetings took place on other college campuses across Minnesota. Awakening also took place among five hundred college students gathered in the summer of 1949 at Forest Home Conference Grounds in Southern California (founded by Henrietta Mears in 1938). Billy Graham and J. Edwin Orr were the principal speakers. Many students were saved while others were revived. They returned to their colleges on fire for God. Other colleges across the country were also being revived.

In 1928, **Henrietta Mears (1890–1963)** became the director of Christian education at First Presbyterian Church in Hollywood, California. The church grew rapidly in attendance from 400 to more than 4,000. Hundreds of young people surrendered to full-time Christian service under her inspiring leadership. She taught the young people to dream big as they prayerfully considered what God had for their lives. She influenced **Bill Bright (1921–2003)** who in 1951 founded **Campus Crusade for Christ, International**, an evangelistic organization that helped lead college students to Christ. Campus Crusade designed "The Four Spiritual Laws," a simple gospel presentation that has been used to lead millions to faith in Jesus.

The most significant name associated with the revival of the 1950s was **William Franklin "Billy" Graham (1918–2018)**. Born in North Carolina, Graham's family attended a small

Presbyterian church in Charlotte. In 1934, some businessmen invited an evangelist named **Mordecai Ham (1877–1961)** to preach a citywide crusade in Charlotte. In that meeting, Billy Graham and his lifelong friend and associate, Grady Wilson, were saved. Billy attended Bob Jones College for a semester and then transferred to Florida Bible Institute in Tampa where in March 1938, he accepted God's call to preach. He preached at various churches and missions in the Tampa area. On December 4, 1938, Graham became a Southern Baptist and was baptized by immersion. He was ordained as a Baptist preacher in 1939. In 1940 he enrolled in Wheaton College in Chicago. There he met Ruth Bell, and they married on August 13, 1943.

Graham became pastor of the Western Springs Church in Chicago. He was invited to preach on a radio program called *Songs in the Night*. There he began working with George Beverly Shea, who became his lifelong partner in ministry. The radio program became popular. Its coordinator, Torrey Johnson, organized a series of youth rallies on Saturday evenings in Chicago and asked Graham to preach. More than 2,800 attended the first meeting. By the twenty-first meeting, a 20,000-seat stadium was necessary to accommodate the crowds. Those meetings were the beginning of the **Youth for Christ (YFC)** organization. Its motto was, "Geared to the Times, but Anchored to the Rock."

Graham resigned his pastorate and began to travel across America, Canada, and England as YFC's evangelist. He met a young music evangelist named Cliff Barrows, and they decided to work together. The Graham-Barrows team went to Great Britain in 1946. In five months, they conducted 360 meetings in twenty-seven cities and towns. Ruth Graham and their children moved to Montreat, North Carolina, to be closer to her parents.

In 1949, Graham's team was invited to lead a crusade in Los Angeles. The crowds numbered about 6,000 nightly. Over the next five weeks, attendance reached more than 9,000 in the final meeting. Several famous people were converted to Christ during that crusade, including renowned Southern California film and radio celebrity, Stuart Hamblen. When Hamblen's friend, actor John Wayne, asked him if he really didn't want to drink beer or whiskey anymore, Hamblen replied, "No John. It's no secret what God can do." Wayne suggested that Hamblen write a song using those words. He did, and it became a Christian favorite. It was entitled (what else?), "It Is No Secret What God Can Do."

National television and radio networks, as well as *Time* and *Newsweek* magazines, covered the Los Angeles Crusade. Within two months, Graham was known across America. In 1950, he held a crusade in Boston which grew so large in attendance it was moved to the Boston Garden for the final service where 16,000 people attended and 10,000 were turned away. In 1957, Graham held a crusade in New York City that lasted sixteen weeks. Over two million people heard him preach at either Madison Square Garden, Yankee Stadium, Central Park, Wall Street, or Brooklyn. One service at Yankee Stadium attracted more than 100,000 people with 20,000 being turned away. During that crusade, more than 55,000 people were converted to Christ in New York City! In 1959, Graham held evangelistic crusades in Australia and New Zealand. More than 3.2 million attended, and more than 150,000 were converted to Christ.

Graham's meetings in America stirred revival fires in churches across the land. Evangelicals who worked together in his citywide crusades learned they could do more for Christ's kingdom when they were united.

There was also a renewed emphasis on Pentecostalism during the 1950s. Revivalist **Oral Roberts (1918–2009)** became known as a faith healer during those years. Roberts used a large tent filled with thousands of seats and a platform from which he preached and ministered. At the end of his message, he invited people to come to the platform so he could pray for their healing. The televised services attracted national attention. Roberts later founded Oral Roberts University and became recognized as a leader in the **charismatic movement**, a new branch of Pentecostalism.

The revival of the 1950s was a genuine, national awakening. American churches experienced tremendous numerical growth and renewed spiritual zeal during that decade.

The Jesus Movement

The last major spiritual awakening in America began toward the end of the 1960s and ended in the early 1970s. It primarily involved the youth in America, many of whom had become dismayed with the youth counterculture. They had experimented with drugs, Eastern religions, the occult, and held frequent anti-establishment demonstrations on college campuses. But it wasn't long until many students in America found what they were looking for in Jesus.

The Setting of the Jesus Movement

The 1960s in America were years of societal chaos. The revival of the 1950s was followed by new social crises. Jorstad labeled this period as "the Tempestuous Sixties."[27] Many in our nation lost their faith in Western theism, the government, and social idealism. There was a categorical shift in the artistic, moral, and religious attitudes of many, particularly among those under thirty. It was a decade of social transition. Young Americans protested causes such as civil rights, the Vietnam War, students' rights, and ecology.

Most Christian churches and denominations in America declined during the 1960s. Church members argued over politics, a lack of relevant preaching, and a lack of genuine fellowship. Young people, along with many adults, were losing their faith in their churches.

While America's youth searched for answers, antiestablishment demonstrations on college campuses proved counterproductive. Four students were killed at Kent State in Ohio by National Guard troops. Political activism wasn't resulting in the rapid changes many young people desired. A sense of foreboding hopelessness prevailed.

Beginnings of the Jesus Movement

Within that drab setting, the Jesus movement began. The awakening did not begin with one person or in a single place. It developed in multiple venues. Jacob dates the beginning of this revival in 1967, although it did not make national headlines until

1970.[28] A Christian "coffeehouse" opened on Haight-Ashbury Street in San Francisco in 1967 that was run by a group of young people who'd been converted to Christ and had abandoned the hippie culture. In 1968, Hollywood Presbyterian Church opened a similar coffeehouse in Southern California called the Salt Company. It offered youth-oriented worship services including upbeat Christian music and a contemporary gospel presentation. Hundreds of teenagers and people in their early twenties walked off the streets into the Salt House. In 1969, Linda Meissner opened a similar coffeehouse to minister to the teenagers of Seattle. Jack Sparks started an organization called the Christian World Liberation Front on the college campus of the University of California at Berkeley. These ministries served as springboards that helped launch a nationwide revival among youth.

Key Leaders of the Jesus Movement

In 1971, the Jesus movement gained national recognition when *Time* magazine gave it major coverage. There were at least three streams of people in the movement: 1) The Jesus People, also called "Jesus Freaks," were the most visible. They dressed like hippies and linked the movement with the youth counterculture. 2) The Straight People composed the largest group in the movement. They worked through local churches and parachurch organizations such as Campus Crusade for Christ, InterVarsity Christian Fellowship, Young Life, and Youth for Christ. 3) The Catholic Pentecostals emerged in 1967. They remained in the Roman Catholic Church but were also actively involved in the Neo-Pentecostal/Charismatic movement.[29]

Several individuals led the Jesus movement. **Chuck Smith (1927–2013)**, pastor of Calvary Chapel in Costa Mesa, California, a suburb of Los Angeles embraced the movement by opening his church's doors and hosting youth services three nights a week. More than two thousand young people with long hair, beards, and blue jeans flooded his church. The services began with a Christian rock group playing contemporary music, followed by praise choruses and a simple Bible study led by Smith. He taught while sitting on a stool.

Calvary Chapel also supported five Christian rock bands, a Bible school, drug abuse programs, beach evangelism (culminating in baptisms in the Pacific Ocean), and the Maranatha Publishing organization. Smith enjoyed being associated with the Jesus movement. He said, "We believe that Calvary Chapel is at the heart of the Jesus Movement. . . . God prepared us, because I preached on agape love for two and a half years. . . . When the kids began to come, we accepted them as they were—long hair and all. We don't ask them to change—it is part of the cleansing work of the Holy Spirit to change them and to get rid of things like drugs, hair, cigarettes and attitudes."[30]

Another strategic leader in the Jesus movement was aforementioned **Jack Sparks**. Sparks was a bearded PhD who founded and led the Christian World Liberation Front (CWLF) at Berkeley, an organization which opposed the left-wing political group on campus called the Berkeley Liberation Movement. The CWLF passed out Christian tracts at the university and also sold Christian books and Bibles to students.

Arthur Blessitt (b. 1940) was another leader in the Jesus movement. On Memorial Day, 1967, Blessitt, along with seventeen young people from five churches, had his first major encounter with a group of street people at a hippie love-in at Griffith Park in Los Angeles. The press covered the event as Blessitt preached about the love of Jesus. Fourteen hippies prayed to receive Christ. News went around the world that the hippies were "getting religion." Blessitt continued to witness to young people on Sunset Strip, as well as to members of the Hell's Angels motorcycle gang. He also opened a coffeehouse on the Strip. In two years, more than 10,000 young people accepted Christ as Savior and Lord. Blessitt became famous for carrying a cross on his shoulder everywhere he preached.

Linda Meissner left her ministry with Teen Challenge in New York after envisioning a massive group of young people marching with Bibles in hand into the city of Seattle. She relocated to Seattle and opened a coffeehouse called The Eleventh Hour, later renaming it the Catacombs. It became the largest Christian coffeehouse in the Jesus movement reaching hundreds of young people for Christ.

Results of the Jesus Movement

The Jesus movement was a genuine spiritual awakening, primarily among the youth of America. From Maine to California, numerous teenagers became "pro Jesus." Christian rock festivals attracted tens of thousands of students. College campus ministries that still exist began during that movement. Asbury College in Wilmore, Kentucky, and other schools experienced revival visitations that caused classes to be temporarily suspended to provide for campus-wide, student-led worship services. Billy Graham affirmed the Jesus movement by saying, "By and large it is a genuine movement of the Spirit of God that is affecting nearly every denomination and social and educational stratum, and is causing discussion from the editorial room of the *New York Times* to the dining room of the White House. . . . Nearly all observers agree that a major spiritual phenomenon is taking shape in young America."[31]

Many Christian denominations that declined numerically in the 1960s saw increases. Southern Baptists experienced their greatest number of baptisms in a consecutive five-year period from 1971 to 1975. Each of those years, more than 400,000 people, many of them teenagers, joined Southern Baptist churches by way of conversion and baptism. Southern Baptists have never had that many baptisms again for that many consecutive years.

Conclusion

At the dawn of the twentieth century, revival winds began to blow in America at the same time spiritual awakening was taking place in Wales. Itinerant evangelists led citywide crusades across America and reached many for Christ. During that revival, the modern Pentecostal movement was also born.

After World War II, Billy Graham helped bring revival, first among young people and then among people of all ages. His citywide crusades led millions to Christ. Television and radio helped spread Graham's gospel message and also brought the healing revivals of Pentecostal evangelist Oral Roberts into America's living rooms.

The final awakening in America was the Jesus movement, which took place in the late 1960s and early 1970s. Focusing on young Americans, it left behind at least three emphases in American Christianity: contemporary Christian music, youth ministry, and parachurch organizations.

Since the mid-1700s, America has experienced six nation-wide revivals. I believe the same God who sovereignly orches-trated those revivals is still alive and able to do the same in our day. Hopefully, these abbreviated accounts of American revivals in this chapter and the previous chapter will prompt us to pray. "O God, tear the heavens open and come down" (cf. Isa. 64:1).

The Lord has done it before. Let's pray He will do it again!

Chapter 8

THE LEADER'S HEART

Before Christian leaders plan and write an order of service, we should humbly bow and pray at the feet of our Leader, Jesus Christ, and ask Him to purify us and to give us His heart. Glorifying and welcoming Him is the goal of our ministry. Before we can *do* right, we must *be* right with Him. What kind of person must we *be* for God to use us to lead in revival?

Years ago, I awoke in the night sensing that God wanted to speak to me. I slipped out of bed, went to my desk at home, and pulled out a piece of paper. Three words came to my mind, and I wrote them down: *humility, hunger,* and *holiness.* I prayed, "Lord, what does this mean?" He didn't answer immediately, but I wasn't anxious. I assumed the significance would come in His timing, and I went back to bed.

A few weeks later, it came to me. Those three words synched perfectly with the revival text of 2 Chronicles 7:14: "[If] my people, who bear my name, *humble* themselves, *pray and seek* my face, and *turn from their evil ways*, then I will hear from heaven,

forgive their sin, and heal their land" (emphasis added). I immediately understood that the three words the Lord shared with
me are His "keys to revival." God opens rivers of living water for
those who *humble* themselves, *hunger* for Him, and seek to live
holy lives. These three "keys" are a pathway for any Christian
who yearns for God's presence.

Humility ("If my people . . . *humble themselves*")

When pride walks into a church, especially into its pulpit,
God walks out. God isn't interested in elevating anyone's ego
or enhancing anyone's resume. God exalts only One—His Son,
Jesus.

That's one reason I've never liked giving grandiose introduc-
tions to guest speakers and musicians who come to our church.
I prefer to say a generic sentence or two: "We're glad to welcome
So-and-so with us today; he faithfully leads at _____. Let's
welcome him to the Bellevue pulpit as he shares (or sings) God's
Word today." The church bulletin may offer more details, but
there's no overemphasis of schools attended, degrees earned,
books written, etc. Those things can easily pull attention away
from Jesus, and we don't need that.

The apostle Peter wrote: "Humble yourselves, therefore,
under the mighty hand of God, so that he may exalt you at the
proper time" (1 Pet. 5:6). When leaders humble themselves,
God exalts them at the appropriate time. But when leaders exalt
themselves, God humbles them. The obvious conclusion is, *let
God do the exalting.* That's why Paul wrote to the Philippians:

"Do nothing out of selfish ambition or conceit, but in humility consider others as more important than yourselves. Everyone should look not to his own interests, but rather to the interests of others. Adopt the same attitude as that of Christ Jesus, who, existing in the form of God, did not consider equality with God as something to be exploited" (Phil. 2:3–6).

What happened when Jesus took the pathway of humility? "For this reason God highly exalted him and gave him the name that is above every name" (v. 9). Jesus took the low position, and God exalted Him!

The night before Jesus died, His disciples argued about who was the greatest among them. Jesus took a bowl and a towel and showed them by washing their feet. Washing feet is humbling. If you've ever washed someone's feet, you understand why people often weep when they do it, and why those whose feet are washed also weep. It's an act of Christlike humility.

When Jesus finished, He asked His disciples: "Do you know what I have done for you?" Had they answered, they probably would have said, *Not really.* Later that evening, Peter still boasted about his courage, only to prove otherwise within a matter of hours.

As Christian leaders, we must remember that all the degrees earned, books read, seminars attended, and expertise we've accumulated are not what we should depend on. We should depend completely on Jesus. He's the one who said: "Blessed are the poor in spirit, for the kingdom of heaven is theirs" (Matt. 5:3). If you are "poor in spirit," you will humbly acknowledge that you cannot be saved, lead a church, be a good family member, or do anything without Him!

In the year 2000, I was diagnosed with a disease called "myasthenia gravis," which literally means "severe muscular weakness." I had double vision and my left eye closed. I was extremely weak for several years. That disease has helped me remain dependent on Jesus. When Paul said, "I came to you in *weakness*" (1 Cor. 2:3, emphasis added), the word *weakness* is the Greek word *asthenia*. Paul said that God blesses and uses people who know they are weak and need the Lord's strength in order to serve Him.

Charles Spurgeon told his young preachers in the late 1800s: be fit for your work, and you will never be out of it. Do not run about inviting yourselves to preach here and there; be more concerned about your ability than your opportunity and more earnest about your walk with God than about either.[32]

Humility is a key that must not be assumed. It's a character trait that no Christian leader dare bypass. God uses humble servants to usher in revival.

Hunger ("If my people . . . *pray and seek my face*")

Christian leaders must also hunger for the Lord and His presence. That necessitates taking in Scripture and praying regularly, every day. Satan attacks every Christian's devotional life by trying to degenerate it into a duty and a routine. When that happens, we know we need to read the Bible and pray, but we have little desire.

92

The office of deacon came about so the apostles could "devote [themselves] to prayer and to the ministry of the word" (Acts 6:4). Many preachers I know are comfortable with "the ministry of the Word" part, but not as many give equal attention to devoting themselves to "prayer."

While we must be disciplined in order to pray, we should also *eagerly* talk with the Lord. Jesus did so even after He had a busy day of ministry that lasted into the night. The next morning, Jesus woke up early and prayed: "Very early in the morning, while it was still dark, he got up, went out, and made his way to a deserted place; and there he was praying" (Mark 1:35).

Some Christians believe revival will come when the LGBTQ community goes back into the closet. I believe revival will come when *the church* gets back into the prayer closet. No Christian leader should try to speak *for* God if he hasn't spent time *with* God in His Word and in prayer. Pastor, read good books written by men, but more so read the Bible that was inspired by God. Don't just read the book of the month. Read the Book of the ages! A Christian leader should read the Bible at the beginning of every day and then pray. God talks to the leader through Scripture, and then the leader talks with God through prayer. We should also be quiet at the end of each prayer time to listen to the still, small voice of God's Spirit.

When I was nineteen, I began memorizing Scripture. For years, I've written Bible verses that I memorize on blank business cards. Over the years I began to write prayer requests on blank business cards, and I pray over them regularly. I also use blank cards by writing out Scripture promises God gives me during my daily Bible reading time, and I pray those promises back to God. Whenever I combine God's Word and prayer, God's peace floods my mind and soul.

I'd be amiss if I didn't mention something important. A leader's prayer life can be derailed if his or her marriage isn't right. In 1 Peter 3:7 we read, "Husbands, in the same way, live with your wives in an understanding way, as with a weaker partner, showing them honor as coheirs of the grace of life, *so that your prayers will not be hindered*" (emphasis added). If I'm not right with my wife, Donna, my prayer life becomes stagnant. Closeness with your spouse is mandatory for any Christian leader to be hungry for God.

As we yearn for God, He blesses our lives and ministry. Hunger and feast upon His presence by taking in Scripture and talking with Him in prayer.

Holiness ("If my people . . . *turn from their evil ways*")

The third key to revival is holiness. God expects His leaders to "turn from their evil ways" and guide others in Christlike holiness. The Bible connects personal holiness to public effectiveness. Notice the last few words from David's prayer of repentance after his immorality with Bathsheba: "God, create a clean heart for me and renew a steadfast spirit within me. Do not banish me from your presence or take your Holy Spirit from me. Restore the joy of your salvation to me, and sustain me by giving me a willing spirit. Then I will teach the rebellious your ways, and *sinners will return to you*" (Ps. 51:10–13, emphasis added).

Only *after* David repented and was cleansed by the Lord would sinners repent. Proverbs 28:13 says: "The one who conceals his sins will not prosper, but whoever confesses and renounces them will find mercy." Christians who try to hide their sins from the Lord undermine their prayers and their service to Him. God's blessings can't be *earned*, but God *blesses* repentance and obedience.

Beneath the Buzz

A leader can get so busy "doing ministry," he can forget his Master and become perfunctory, just going through the motions. Being alone and intimate with Jesus brings back the Spirit's fruit of "love, joy, [and] peace" (i.e., Christlikeness; Gal. 5:22). God commands Christian leaders "to be conformed to the image of his Son" (Rom. 8:29).

A growing church program can create a fabricated buzz. A "successful" pastor, like a successful athlete, should NOT read his own press clippings. Growing church numbers aren't necessarily synonymous with God's approval of our lives and ministries. The ultimate reward is to one day stand before Jesus and hear His, "Well done." That won't come automatically by "building a great church." But it will come to all Christian leaders whose "goal is to know him and the power of his resurrection and the fellowship of his sufferings, being conformed to his death, assuming that I will somehow reach the resurrection from among the dead" (Phil. 3:10–11). Ministry that can be explained by human effort isn't good enough. Christian leaders need God's supernatural power.

Regardless of how well we think we know the Lord, there's always more of Him to acknowledge and embrace. Leader, worshipping and seeking Jesus's face was where your ministry began. Before the appointments, budgets, meetings, sermons, and denominational gatherings, it was just you, Jesus, your Bible, and your prayer closet. He was all you had back then. And He's all you need now.

Let's get back to Jesus by drawing close to Him through *humility, hunger,* and *holiness.* He's ready and able to bless us more than we can fathom.

Chapter 9

ATTRACTING GOD'S PRESENCE

When God sent Jesus to earth to bring salvation to mankind, He didn't send Him to a king's palace. Instead, Jesus was born to a village girl named Mary. The first public announcement about Him went to rural shepherds, not to the social elites.

Similarly, when God visits us today, He doesn't have to show up at grandiose, Gothic cathedrals or human-focused denominational conferences. Whenever God visits our planet, it's a huge step down from heaven's glory. So, what kind of atmosphere could we possibly assemble that could make the God of the universe feel welcome?

The previous chapter described the heart of the Christian leader who seeks to attract God's presence: humility, hunger, and holiness. Let's expand on those points with the marks of all who seek God's presence: prayer, tithing, fasting, repentance, worship, and unity.

Years ago, my friend, the late Don Miller, spoke about "living under an open heaven." I thought, *That's what I want! No barriers between me and God!* Miller, the greatest prayer warrior I've ever known, pointed to Luke's account of Jesus's baptism that says, "As he was praying, heaven opened, and the Holy Spirit descended on him in a physical appearance like a dove" (Luke 3:21–22). *The heavens opened, and God's Spirit came down!*

That's what all of us should desire. But what attracts the presence of God?

Prayer

On earth Jesus was God incarnate. Yet He prayed constantly. He prayed when He was tempted to sin (Matt. 4:1), early in the morning (Mark 1:35), in the middle of the day (Luke 5:16), before He chose His disciples (Luke 6:12), and in Gethsemane before He was arrested (Matt. 26:36). Jesus also prayed while He was on the cross. Out of the seven statements Jesus made on the cross, three were prayers. Jesus's three "cross prayers" were: 1) "Father, forgive them, because they do not know what they are doing" (Luke 23:34); 2) "My God, my God, why have you abandoned me?" (Mark 15:34); and 3) "Father, into your hands I entrust my spirit" (Luke 23:46). Our Lord began and ended His suffering on the cross with prayer.

Jesus also prayed in His resurrected state. On Easter night with the Emmaus disciples, "he took the bread, *blessed* and broke it, and gave it to them" (Luke 24:30, emphasis added). Our resurrected Lord would not even put a morsel of bread in His mouth without first thanking His Father for it!

No wonder the only thing Jesus's disciples ever asked Him to teach them was, "Lord, teach us to pray" (Luke 11:1). They had listened to Jesus pray and had watched Him prioritize prayer in His life and ministry. They understood that answered prayer was the source of His strength and wisdom, and they wanted to be like Him!

Amazingly, Jesus still prays *today*! Hebrews 7:25 says, "Therefore, he is able to save completely those who come to God through him, since *he always lives to intercede for them*" (emphasis added).

Jesus's disciples followed His example by praying. After His ascension to heaven, they went to the upper room, and "they all were continually united in prayer" (Acts 1:14). They prayed for ten days until God's Spirit fell upon them. Peter preached one sermon and 3,000 were saved. If we prayed like they did, more lost people would be saved.

Wherever prayer focuses, God's power falls. God's "house" isn't primarily for preaching and meeting; it's for praying. We need Christians who will pray passionately with tears, like Jesus: "During his earthly life, *he offered prayers and appeals with loud cries and tears* to the one who was able to save him from death, and he was heard because of his reverence" (Heb. 5:7, emphasis added). When was the last time you prayed "with loud cries and tears"?

Many of us today don't pray fervently because we're so "comfortable." Our prayers must be passionate if we want to attract God's presence.

Tithing

The Bible says in Malachi 3:10, "'Bring the full tenth into the storehouse so that there may be food in my house. Test me in this way,' says the LORD of Armies. 'See if I will not *open the floodgates of heaven and pour out a blessing for you without measure*'" (emphasis added). God promises to bless tithing even though some Christians dismiss it saying it was exclusively an Old Testament concept. But when did the New Testament ever *lower* an Old Testament standard? If the Old Testament saints gave 10 percent, perhaps Christians should give even more.

Jesus affirmed tithing when He said to the Pharisees, "You pay a tenth of mint, dill, and cumin, and yet you have neglected the more important matters of the law—justice, mercy, and faithfulness. These things should have been done *without neglecting the others*" (Matt. 23:23, emphasis added). Here Jesus taught that Christians should tithe while they also extend justice, mercy, and faithfulness.

Many churches engage in fundraisers instead of tithing. When churches have car washes, peddle merchandize door-to-door, and sell raffle tickets, they're asking the world to support God's church. That's a poor witness and a sad substitute for the biblical practice of tithing. God called nontithers thieves who are cursed. "You are suffering under *a curse*, yet you—the whole nation—are still *robbing* me!" (Mal. 3:9, emphasis added). You can't rob God and also be intimate with Him.

Christians can't afford *not* to tithe because it opens up the windows of heaven and brings down God's blessings. Church members who want God's presence in their midst should tithe.

Fasting

When your hunger for God exceeds your hunger for food, you'll forgo the second to satisfy the first. Fasting is part of New Testament Christianity. Fasting puts your prayers into "high gear." I don't understand how a car works, but I drive one every day. And I don't understand why God blesses fasting, but I know He does.

Queen Esther fasted (Esther 4:15–17), Daniel fasted wearing "sackcloth and ashes" (Dan. 9:3), and Jesus fasted (Matt. 4:2). Jesus also told His disciples that some demonic strongmen and strongholds can only be overcome through fasting (Matt. 17:21).

Fasting is one of the best ways to show God that you are serious about experiencing His presence and power. Fasting sends the message to heaven that you want Him even more than your daily food. I can personally attest that God blesses fasting and that it attracts His presence.

Repentance

The closer we get to God, the more plainly we see our sins. The spotlight of His holiness grows brighter, exposing the darkness of our disobedience. To *repent* means to "turn around." The sooner you repent, the more intimate you will be with Jesus. Peter said in Acts 3:19–20: "Therefore *repent and turn back*, so that your sins may be wiped out, that seasons of refreshing may come from the presence of the Lord" (emphasis added). If Christians are carrying the heavy baggage of unconfessed, unforsaken sin in their lives, they need to repent immediately. God hates sin! Proverbs 3:32 says: "For the devious are detestable to the LORD, but he is a friend to the upright."

Some Christians in America think, *We're the good guys, the red white and blue. God would never mess up our party.* I'm an American, but God isn't. If Americans refuse to repent, God owes us nothing. I'm convinced America needs God a lot more than He needs America.

My wife, Donna, went on a mission trip to Romania. During the Communist era, Christians there were ridiculed as *pocaiți*, which means "repenters." That's how God sees all real Christians—as repenters. In America, we call ourselves "believers," which means we affirm a set of doctrines. It's mainly mental, rational, and propositional. Perhaps we should become *repenters* instead of mere believers! Your repentance will attract God's presence.

Worship

Worship plays an important role in laying out the welcome mat *ahead of* God's manifest presence. In 2 Chronicles 20, King Jehoshaphat and the nation of Judah were about to be massacred by the armies of three nations. Jehoshaphat "was afraid, and he resolved to seek the LORD. Then he proclaimed a fast for all Judah, who gathered to seek the LORD" (vv. 3–4). Jehoshaphat and his people fasted, prayed, and worshipped the Lord. His army kept singing and praising the Lord as they approached the battlefield. Suddenly, the enemy coalition turned against one another. By the time Judah's army arrived, the dead bodies of their enemies were lying across the landscape. God showed up and showed off, so to speak, when His people worshipped Him! The people of Judah praised God in advance, and He took care of everything.

Similarly, when Paul and Silas were in jail at Philippi, they stayed awake that night praying and worshipping God. That's when He set them free! "About midnight Paul and Silas were praying and singing hymns to God" (Acts 16:25). God sent an earthquake and set everyone free!

When we fail to worship God, we forfeit the power of praise. But when we praise and worship the Lord, He does awesome things. Worshipping God attracts His presence!

Unity

The final thing we will mention that welcomes God's presence is unity. When God's people are in harmony with one another, the Lord comes to us in power because we're flowing in the same direction with Him. Psalm 133 has only three verses, but they vividly describe the benefits of Christian unity: "How delightfully good when brothers live together in harmony! It is like fine oil on the head, running down on the beard, running down Aaron's beard onto his robes. It is like the dew of Hermon falling on the mountains of Zion. For there the LORD has appointed the blessing—life forevermore" (vv. 1–3).

In this psalm, unity is likened to the anointing oil of the Jewish high priest. It started flowing at the top of the priest's head, then down his beard and robe, and finally onto the ground. Second, unity is likened to the water runoff from Mount Hermon in northern Israel. At 9,200-plus feet, it's the only snow-capped mountain in the Middle East. Today, it produces 40 percent of Israel's freshwater supply as its streams run down into the Sea of Galilee and feed into the Jordan River. *Jor* in Hebrew means "descend from." "Dan" was the northernmost tribe of Israel. So the river's name simply means "descending from Dan," which is where the water originates.

The psalmist made these two images into a picture of spiritual unity. Both start at the top and flow downward. That's how unity works in a church. It starts by flowing at the top through the pastor and staff to the lay leadership and finally to the rest of the congregation.

The Holy Spirit is quenched when church members resist the God-ordained leadership of a church. The Lord calls pastors to lead, deacons to serve, and everyone to relate peacefully in His churches. If there is tension and fighting anywhere, God's anointing won't flow. Many churches are like the people in the book of Judges: "In those days there was no king [leader] in Israel; everyone did whatever seemed right to him" (21:25).

Baptists struggle in this area. We're known for contentious business meetings. We don't need to air our dirty laundry in front of everybody, especially new Christians. Acts 15 shows a better way. Leaders came together behind closed doors, hashed out their church's problems privately, and then made a unified announcement to the whole church. That's unity God's way. The Lord blesses unity with His manifest presence.

Scripture wholeheartedly affirms that fervent prayer, obedient tithing, selfless fasting, honest repentance, sincere worship, and humble unity are proven, biblical disciplines and attributes that attract God's manifest presence into our lives and into our churches.

Chapter 10

FLOW, NOT SHOW

When our children were young, we would attend their variety shows at school. Donna and I would sit with all the other parents, eager to see what our kiddos had cooked up. They'd sing, dance, tell stories, etc. When it was over, we wrapped our arms around them and said, "You did great! You were awesome! We're so proud of you. Let's get ice cream on the way home!"

That's good when it comes to children putting on a program. But there's a huge difference between a "variety show" and a Savior-focused worship experience.

If all we do when we plan a church service is tape together a crowd-pleasing lineup—a welcome, some fast songs, a slow song, announcements, a choir song, a video clip, a sermon, a baptism or Communion observance, and a closing prayer—all to fit perfectly in sixty or seventy-five minutes, we've badly missed the mark. We've forgotten our true Audience, the Lord Jesus. We've moved from an *encounter* with God to an *event*.

Many church services today feel choppy. Just when the spirit of worship really begins to breathe in a worship service, we interrupt it with an offering or an announcement. We shoot ourselves in the foot. The protocol of *Okay, what's next on the list?* takes over.

A Seamless Core

If you visit our church on a Sunday morning, you will experience *one continuous flow* throughout the worship service. Our goal is as little disruption as possible. This can look different for any church, of course, but I want to share some of how we do what we do in the spirit of offering some practical inspiration. At the moment we start, I say to the congregation, "Good morning. Let's gather in groups for prayer. Find two or three people nearby, and one of you start praying." Immediately multiple Christians gather in small groups and pray out loud simultaneously. When I say "Amen," we begin a praise song. The band and singers join in as we sing with the words on the screen. With screens, everyone can see the words clearly, and the transition from song to song is smooth. The minister of music seamlessly leads the congregation through each song without any interruption.

After we sing, we celebrate baptism. Everyone in the sanctuary remains standing. The staff member who baptizes the new believers shares the name of each baptismal candidate along with a brief testimony of how that person came to salvation in Christ. When the person comes up out of the water, the entire congregation claps and shouts with amens and hallelujahs! After baptism, still standing, we reengage in singing.

After the praise songs are sung, I preach from a biblical text. Normally, I walk verse *by* verse through the Scripture for the day, explaining, illustrating, and applying the text. Occasionally, I'll preach a topical sermon using multiple Bible verses that focus on one topic in a "verse *with* verse" method. But normally, I preach verse *by* verse.

When I preach, I don't waste time with excessive humor or personal tales from the past week. I go straight to the Scripture. I don't try to be cute and clever. Our people desire to hear from God's Word, not a pastor's comedy routine. Charles Spurgeon put it vividly when he said to his young preachers, "As long as the guests get the spiritual meat, the waiter at the table may be happy to be forgotten."[33]

Once again, screen projection helps engage the worshippers. Listeners become "seers" as my main sermon points and the supporting Scriptures appear in visual form. Also, when I ask the congregation to read a portion of Scripture out loud simultaneously, the screens unify everyone on one Bible translation, even though individuals brought different Bible versions to church.

At the end of the sermon, I invite Christians to prayerfully apply the theme of the text to their lives. Then I always give non-Christians the opportunity to be born again by inviting them to *repent* of their sins, *believe* savingly in Jesus, and *receive* Him as their Lord and Savior. Then, just as a pastor at a wedding leads a young couple in their wedding vows, I lead those who want to be saved in a prayer to repent, believe, and receive Jesus.

As we sing our final worship song, I invite people to come to the front where our pastors and other counselors are waiting. Those who've prayed to receive Christ come and tell someone what they've done. We counsel them to take the next step that follows salvation, which is baptism. We also counsel with those who would like to start the process of joining our church.

During this time of invitation, we pray for sick people to be healed, according to James 5:14–16: "Is anyone among you sick? He should call for the elders of the church, and they are to pray over him, anointing him with oil in the name of the Lord. The prayer of faith will save the sick person, and the Lord will raise him up; if he has committed sins, he will be forgiven. Therefore, confess your sins to one another and pray for one another, so that you may be healed. The prayer of a righteous person is very powerful in its effect."

The Lord still saves, delivers, and heals. As my personal physician (who also serves as a deacon at our church) says, "God can heal people physically by medicine, miracle, or both." Every Sunday at Bellevue during our invitation time, our pastors lay hands on sick people, anoint them with oil, and pray for them to be healed. Some are healed and some aren't. I simply say, "It's our job to ask, and it's God's job to answer. And no matter how He answers, we'll give Him the glory."

I also extend an invitation to those who are sensing that God might want them to serve in full-time, vocational ministerial service. I ask them to come and let one of our pastors pray with them and help them move forward in that process. Many have surrendered to preach the gospel as an evangelist, pastor, or missionary. Others have felt led of the Lord to serve in other leadership roles such as leading worship, discipleship, student ministry, ministry to singles, and so on. We simply call out those whom God has called.

After the invitation, we encourage people to give their tithes and offerings either online or by using receptacles around the campus. We have chosen not to pass offering plates around because the logistics can feel like an interruption. Then I invite our guests to meet briefly with me outside the sanctuary at the conclusion of the service. As Donna and I walk out, announcements are shown on the screens. Our associate pastor closes with prayer, and everyone is dismissed. The Sunday worship service at your church might look different, of course, but I hope you get the spirit of our pursuit: a steady flow with as few interruptions in the worship service as possible.

How Much Control?

I believe God's Spirit can guide us on Thursday morning at a worship planning meeting as well as during a Sunday morning service. But what if we, in our humanity, forgot something? What if the Holy Spirit had an idea He couldn't get us to listen to when we were planning earlier in the week? What if He wanted us to go in a different direction, and we were spiritually deaf?

Worship leaders often get in trouble when they write an order of service and behave as if it's cast in stone. They prefer to do only that which is preprogrammed. If the order says they're going to sing a song, then they will sing it. They become slaves to the script.

I believe pastors should be like quarterbacks who can call an audible now and then. Calling an audible means the quarterback is responding to new conditions on the field that were not present the last moment the team discussed the next play. Pastors likewise need to be free to say, "I'm sensing that the Spirit of God would have us go in a different direction." That ought not to dismay the minister of music or anyone else on the platform. Worship programs should always be subject to change.

At Bellevue, I work with wonderful ministers of music who are spiritually sensitive and flexible. If I sing a song that wasn't on the "plan," our musicians are capable and willing to play the additional song and go with it. There's no ego involved in me or the musicians. No one gets their feelings hurt. The worship service is not about us anyway. It's about Jesus!

There have been times in a service when I've strongly sensed the Lord saying to my heart, *Pray for people who are discouraged.* Or, *Give a chance for people who are sick to be prayed for right now.* I've said to the congregation, "If you're hurting in some way today, either in your body or in your spirit, come to the altar and we'll pray for you." Those have turned out to be precious times of intercession and ministry.

In trying to be led by the Holy Spirit in a service, I'm sure we've missed God's direction from time to time. But God allows for human misjudgments. Still, I'd rather seek His guidance and make an error than to say, "We've written our order of service, and that's that, period."

Pastors can be like pharaohs sometimes. We can declare how things are going to proceed and veto certain expressions because "we don't do things like that at this church." Meanwhile, God is saying, "Let My people go that they may worship Me! They want to pour out their love to Me. Stop blocking their way. Release My people!"

If somebody is genuinely worshipping the Lord by lifting their hands or saying amen, I'm not going to tell them to stop. Some of them are wired to be more expressive than others, and that's okay. I want people to connect with God.

Too often, worship services are like going to a ballet performance. The actors on stage are all highly trained, splendidly dressed, and wonderfully synchronized as they go through their leaps and twirls. But the congregation sits there knowing that everything is canned. Nobody is going to move a muscle or do anything that hasn't been rehearsed several times.

Personally, I prefer to do church like a football game. Yes, there are rules and boundaries, but you never know what's going to happen. You're on the edge of your seat with anticipation.

Jesus was the most unpredictable person who ever lived. People never knew what He was going to say or do. That's one reason they found Him so fascinating. His ultimate surprise was His resurrection. Suddenly, He was alive again!

Does "calling an audible" on Sunday morning ever mess up the time schedule? Possibly, but so what? Again, people at a football game don't complain when it goes into overtime. Any relationship that is chained to a clock is stunted. When God shows up in a worship service, He forgets about time, and so should we.

So what if the next service has to start ten minutes late. We can adjust for that. Whatever keeps us from following God must be dealt with. People in the congregation can tell when we've got one eye on the clock and the other on the order of service.

Notice what happened when revival hit in Nehemiah's day: "While they stood in their places, they read from the book of the law of the LORD their God for a fourth of the day and spent another fourth of the day in confession and worship of the LORD their God" (Neh. 9:3). That's how it goes in God's presence. That's why eternity will be timeless. If we can't handle more than an hour in church, what makes us think we'll like heaven? In fact, what makes us think we'll go there at all?

Sadly, many evangelical seminaries today don't teach students who are training to be lead pastors how to lead a worship service. They spend time teaching Hebrew, Greek, theology, and church history but ignore corporate worship that is sensitive to the leading of the Holy Spirit. Pastors end up having to learn that on their own. I'm not criticizing, just offering some coaching to my fellow pastors.

Pastors, when it comes to worship services, prioritize flow, not show. Pray for wisdom to hear God's voice as you plan a worship service and as you participate in and lead a worship service.

Entering into the flow of God's presence is a high privilege we should embrace. I'm just grateful the Lord has agreed to meet with us!

Chapter 11

MUSIC: THE AGONY AND THE ECSTASY

Henry Wadsworth Longfellow, the great American poet wrote in the 1830s, "Music is the universal language of mankind."[34] That may be true, but in many churches, music is also the universal *aggravation* of the brethren.

Christians can get emotional about church music styles. Many churches engage in musical *wars*. They struggle over formats, styles, rhythms, volumes, and newer music versus the old. Which instruments shall we use? How fast can we play them? Can any good thing come out of a guitar or a hymnal?

Some members are attracted to contemporary movements in music and feel impatient with the slowness of change. Members who prefer more traditional music feel scorned and abandoned. The older we get, the less we enjoy change. We like things to stay the way they've been. Younger people, however, favor innovation. They don't understand why "Amazing Grace" means so much to Granddad. That's because they weren't present that Sunday night when he was born again in a worship service while it was being sung. Neither party is wrong; they're just coming from different angles.

So, what do we do with our differences? How do we calm down the "worship wars"?

The Missing Notes

Here is how I have chosen, as a pastor, to work through this issue. I believe that you and I don't need to fuss about church music because we're not the Audience, remember? Singing in the house of God is not primarily for our benefit. Rather, it's an offering to the Lord. The main point is to please Him, not ourselves. If He's happy with our praise, that's all that really matters.

In the middle of the Bible, God gave us a divinely inspired hymnal with 150 different songs—*with just the words*. That hymnal is the book of Psalms. It contains no notes, harmonies, rhythms, instrumentation, or chord charts. I believe the Lord left the music out on purpose. He wanted us to value the important part—the content. God also left out the music so each culture and generation could "sing a new song to the LORD" (Ps. 96:1). He welcomes each style as long as it comes from a worshipful heart.

We should focus on worshipping the Lord rather than having our own way. Romans 12:10 says, "Love one another deeply as brothers and sisters. Take the lead in honoring one another." We're to prefer and value the view of others when it comes to church music (or anything else). Philippians 2:3 says, "Do nothing out of selfish ambition or conceit, but in humility consider others as more important than yourselves." You might not think of these texts in connection with worship music, but they certainly apply.

Christ's church is a rare *mix* of ages and stages. Most societal groupings are designed for a specific musical *niche*. That's why radio stations offer country music, news/talk, classical music, rock and roll, oldies, rhythm and blues, Latino music, jazz, and others. Restaurants do the same with food: Italian, Asian, French, fast-food, fine dining . . . you name it. We're spoiled in America. We look for goods and services tailored *just for us*.

Then on Sunday, we come to church. We are by definition *the family* of God, which means we're not all alike. Some are male, others are female. Some are younger, others are older. Some are financially comfortable; others struggle to pay their light bill. Some went to college; others went straight to work. Yet we are all in the same place at the same time trying to worship the same God. How can we all get along?

What if a rich entrepreneur told you he'd pick up the tab for a musical concert in the city park if you'd plan it—the only requirement being that everybody from age eight to eighty-eight would love every song?! The teenagers, old folks, PhDs, dropouts, Southerners, Yankees, African Americans, whites, Asians, and Latinos—they'd all be there from all over town, and you'd have to please them all. You'd say, "Impossible!"

That's often the way it is in our worship services. Every worship leader knows what I'm talking about. If the goal is to satisfy everyone, the future is doomed. We must change the standard.

Early in my ministry here at Bellevue, I preached a sermon from Acts 2:42–47 titled, "I Believe in the Church." The passage describes the Jerusalem congregation, but it doesn't say much about their music. All it says is they were "praising God." I told our congregation, "We have several thousand people here today, and I have no intention of dividing our church into age brackets because of music. I want children to sit with their grandparents. We all need to be under the same roof together in the Lord's presence. So, in every service, we'll sing hymns, and we'll also sing modern worship songs. They'll all be theologically sound and Christ centered. We're not going to focus on what we *don't* like. We're going to focus on what we *do* like—which is one another! I may not love a particular beat, but I love *you*. And if you worship the Lord through a particular song, whether I like it or not, I'll be happy. Everyone is going to have to bend a little. If you don't like a particular song, just stay calm and wait a few minutes. The next one is likely to be more engaging."

Jesus said, "A disciple in the kingdom of heaven is like the owner of a house who brings out of his storeroom treasures new and old" (Matt. 13:52). Some church songs are older; others are new. Let's use them all. Some might say, "You can't teach an old dog new tricks." Thank the Lord, Christians aren't dogs. We'll love one another by singing a new song to the Lord together.

The church was never meant to be your personal jukebox. We can pick out the songs we prefer the rest of the week. With an iPhone, you can play your favorites to your heart's content. But in God's house, we're offering up praise for Someone Else.

C. S. Lewis surrendered to Christ at the age of thirty. He was already a brilliant professor of English literature at Oxford. Blending into a local church's worship was hard for him:

> I thought that I could do it on my own, by retiring to my room and reading theology, and wouldn't go to the church and Gospel Halls. . . . I disliked very much their hymns which I considered to be fifth-rate poems set to sixth-rate music. But as I went on I saw the merit of it. I came up against different people of quite different outlooks and different education, and then gradually my conceit just began peeling off. I realized that the hymns (which were just sixth-rate music) were, nevertheless, being sung with devotion and benefit by an old saint in elastic-side boots in the opposite pew, and then you realize that you aren't fit to clean those boots. It gets you out of your solitary conceit.[35]

Art for His Sake, Not Ours

No one knows what style of music is in heaven. I tease my church by saying, "You'd better be glad *I'm* not in charge of selecting all the music here and in heaven. We'd be listening to bluegrass every week! How many of you would like that?" I usually get two hands waving, as everybody laughs. When Donna and I get in my SUV, she says, "Turn it off." I reply, "You haven't even heard anything yet!" She replies, "I know it's there. The minute you turn the key, I'm going to get blasted by Flatt and Scruggs." I smile. Some folks just don't get it.

But when we worship the Lord, the priority is not really what I, or Donna, or anybody else likes. We're to submit our personal tastes to the greater purpose of worship and join together as we honor and exalt the true Audience. If He is pleased, all is well.

Like all art forms, music changes. "Amazing Grace" is a great hymn from John Newton who lived in the 1700s. Some sing it slowly, while others sing it with a more contemporary beat. Other hymns are now being massaged similarly by adjusting the melody or adding an all-new bridge passage or coda at the end. The best of the old is preserved as new touches bring enrichment.

If you think about it, all hymns were "contemporary" at one point. There was a day when "Amazing Grace" and "Joyful, Joyful We Adore Thee" were brand-new, edgy songs. But through the centuries they've become classics. The same will happen to some of today's praise songs. Most will be forgotten, but a few will become "old favorites."

It's a lot like your car. No one actually drives a "new car." That's because it becomes a "used car" one second after you drive it off the dealer's lot. In the same way, every song we sing is "old" in human terms; some are just further along than others.

A hymnal is a collection of time-tested songs from the past. It's not to be compared with the latest sampler of contemporary music. That's apples versus oranges. In the 1700s, Charles Wesley wrote thousands of hymns, but we only sing a handful of them today: "O for a Thousand Tongues," "Hark, the Herald Angels

Sing," "Christ the Lord Is Risen Today," and a few others. Most of his other hymns are long gone. We've kept the best and laid aside the rest. That happens to all songwriters. It will happen to today's Christian songs as well. The wheat will be sifted from the chaff. No songwriter produces wheat every time.

The age of a song is irrelevant to its value. What matters is whether it lifts up the Lord and worshippers will still use it to exalt Him. We'll do well to use songs from a wide variety of sources, regardless of the copyright date.

See the River

Think of worship as a boat trip down a beautiful river. The psalmist actually wrote, "There is a river—its streams delight the city of God, the holy dwelling place of the Most High." (Ps. 46:4). If you and I are involved in bringing gladness to the heart of God, every minute we spend studying the boat, the engine, or the rudder is a moment lost from the scenery of the river. As long as we're thinking about the *music* and its contours, we're not thinking about the Lord.

We don't truly worship until we get *beyond* the music. We must rise above the notes and rhythm patterns and become "lost in wonder, love, and praise," as Wesley wrote at the end of his hymn "Love Divine, All Loves Excelling." We don't need to fuss over an art form. We're the church of the living God, not a music society. Music, like technology, makes a wonderful servant but a terrible master.

Perhaps the most musical of all the Psalms is the last one, Psalm 150. It mentions using several orchestra instruments, from trumpets, to pipes, to "loud cymbals." It ends with this stirring finale: "Let everything that breathes praise the LORD" (v. 6).

Notice, it does *not* say, "Let everything that breathes criticize the music." God didn't give us breath to complain. If we're breathing, we should use that breath to praise God! That's the purpose of worship music and the solution for the "music wars" of our day.

Chapter 12

PRAYING TOGETHER

Praying with others is important. Few Bible-believing Christians are against corporate prayer, but how many are fervently *for* it? Do all those who *believe* in prayer pray regularly with other Christians? When we gather to worship the Lord corporately, prayer should be more than a "silencer" to get the crowd to quiet down at the start of a worship service. Praying together must become the heart of every church.

While many churches seem indifferent about prayer, God isn't. Just as a parent loves to hear his children's voices, God loves to hear His assembled children talk with Him. Some Christians say glibly, "God's going to do whatever God's going to do. Prayer doesn't change anything. It just changes the person who prays." That's just wrong. God will do some things whether we pray or not. There are also things God won't do no matter how much we pray. But there are some things God will do only if we pray.

Jesus clearly took prayer seriously. He said we need "to pray always and not give up" (Luke 18:1) in His story about the persistent widow and the obstinate judge (cf. Luke 18:1–8). The widow's persistence produced results, and so does a Christian's persistence in prayer today.

The devil also takes prayer seriously. Jesus said in Mark 9:29, "This kind can come out by nothing but prayer." Jesus was saying some demonic spirits are so powerful they can only be overcome by means of prayer. What you do on your knees in prayer pushes back the prince of darkness, his demonic forces, and their diabolic agenda.

I preached a sermon years ago entitled "Are You Known in Hell?" My text was Acts 19:11–17, the story about some unbelievers in Ephesus who tried to cast out a demon without the power of genuine prayer. The evil spirit gave them an old-fashioned "whipping" by attacking and overpowering them as it snarled, "I know Jesus, and I recognize Paul—but who are you?" (v. 15). The devil and his minions wisely fear Jesus, the Son of God, and they also know about praying Christians like the apostle Paul. Prayerless people are no threat to Satan, but a praying Christian is.

Heaven knows who you are. Do demons?

More Than a Gift

Prayer isn't a spiritual gift that God gives only to "super" Christians. Paul commanded the entire Ephesian church to "pray at all times in the Spirit with every prayer and request, and stay alert with all perseverance and intercession for all the saints" (Eph. 6:18). Prayer is every Christian's responsibility.

When preaching evangelistically, we often say "the ground is level at the cross," meaning that God invites everyone to be saved. May I add that the ground is also level at the prayer closet. God invites every Christian to pray. A brand-new Christian can talk to God as directly as someone who's been saved forty years. You don't work your way up a seniority ladder in prayer. God desires to hear from every believer.

In college I took voice lessons. On the first day the teacher said, "You're singing wrong because you're not breathing diaphragmatically. You're breathing with your chest, not your stomach." He taught me how to breathe correctly so I could sing correctly. Soon he was saying, "Now you're breathing with your diaphragm. And that's how to breathe when you sing." Then he said something I'll never forget: *"You can't sing until you learn how to breathe."*

Over the years, I've related the parallel between breathing and singing to praying and preaching. *You can't preach until you know how to pray.* If you don't pray right, you won't preach right, you won't live right, and you won't do right. Prayer is spiritual breathing. If you don't talk *with* God in prayer, you won't be able to effectively talk *for* God when you preach. Every Christian needs to breathe spiritually by praying. Likewise, a church will only grow strong and healthy when it engages in the inhale-exhale rhythm of prayer. Mere programs and elaborate systems won't cut it long term. A church will either pray, or it will die.

Prayer isn't just for the experts (i.e., "prayer warriors"). Prayer is for all Christians.

Prayer in the Sanctuary

Every Sunday morning at seven, a group of our staff members gather at Bellevue to pray over the worship center. We go row by row, laying our hands on each seat, asking God to make Himself real to whoever sits there that day. We ask God to save, heal, deliver, set free, and speak to individuals. We then gather at the altar area and pray that people will come to Christ in salvation. We pray over the pulpit asking God to bless the preaching that day. That Sunday morning prayer time takes half an hour, and it's a precious time. I can't think of anything more important for our staff leaders to do. We're turning on the "prayer conditioning" in the building as we pray. From there, our staff members scatter across our campus to get ready for their various duties. But we've started our day calling out to God in prayer.

During our invitation time after my sermon, we have trained prayer counselors standing across the front. I say to the congregation, "If you have a need today, come and pray with one of us." Folks stream forward, take someone's hand, and share their deepest needs. The counselors listen quietly and then go straight to God in prayer. While we pray together, the rest of the congregation sings and worships the Lord. How many problems and burdens are alleviated simply by praying together in a church service? We "do not have because [we] do not ask" (James 4:2).

God is our loving, attentive, heavenly Father. He invites us to nestle up close to Him and receive His love. What better place to do that than in church? One reason the Jewish rabbis hated Jesus was that He sounded too intimate with God. Seldom in the

Old Testament had God been spoken of as "Father." But Jesus frequently referred to God as His Father. When the Pharisees challenged His credentials, He replied:

> "Even in your law it is written that the testimony of two witnesses is true. I am the one who testifies about myself, and the Father who sent me testifies about me."
>
> Then they asked him, "Where is your Father?"
>
> "You know neither me nor my Father," Jesus answered. "If you knew me, you would also know my Father." (John 8:17–19)

People today are starving for the loving embrace of a father. The more we realize what a good Father the Lord is to us, the more we will talk with Him in prayer.

Another great occasion for me to pray with others comes as I walk slowly through the crowds before or after the worship service. Inevitably, somebody comes up to me and says, "Would you pray for me? I'm having medical tests this week," or "My marriage isn't doing well." I've learned to listen and then say, "Let's pray right now." I take them by the hand and intercede with them on the spot. Why not? The church is a house of prayer. That way the person knows I'm taking their need seriously. It's better than saying, "Yes, I'll pray for you," and never getting around to it. Better to pray immediately. I've prayed for people in airports, parking lots, Walmart, and many other places. Just today I prayed for a lady at Costco who had a spiritual need.

The Lord is available to hear us, and the person is standing right there—so why delay?

Prayer beyond the Sanctuary

Some people in church are nervous about praying in a large group because they worry about "not sounding right" when they talk with God. They need instruction about prayer in a non-threatening environment. I teach prayer in my weekly discipleship group as I mentor young men on our staff. Every eighteen months, I take four to five young men, and we meet once a week. We read the Bible, share what God is teaching us, read and discuss good Christian books, and we pray. This has turned out to be a great mentoring time. The best way to learn how to pray is to pray with someone who is comfortable praying. Prayer is as much caught as it is taught.

On occasions, I've also taught classes at our church on "How to Spend an Hour with God in Prayer." People say, "An hour—are you kidding? I'd run out of topics in ten minutes." Yet those same people have no problem watching television for an hour. In the garden of Gethsemane, Jesus said to His disciples, "Couldn't you stay awake with me one hour? Stay awake and pray" (Matt. 26:40–41). He was saying, *Guys, an hour in prayer is no big deal.*

If you're married, think back to your engagement period. An hour spent with the one you love was like a snap of the finger. It was midnight before you knew it. Why should an hour with God be any different?

Here's a simple guide to pray for an hour . . .

How to Spend an Hour with God

- Enter into God's presence with singing or silence (5 minutes)
- Praise God according to His names in Scripture (15 minutes)
  - Jehovah-Jireh—The Lord My Provider
  - Jehovah-Nissi—The Lord My Banner (who protects me)
  - Jehovah-Rapha—The Lord Who Heals Me
  - Jehovah-Shammah—The Lord Who Is Present with Me
  - Jehovah-Shalom—The Lord My Peace
  - Jehovah-Tsidkenu—The Lord My Righteousness
  - Jehovah-Rohi—The Lord My Shepherd
  - Jehovah-Makadesh—The Lord Who Sanctifies Me
- Thank God for His Blessings (5 minutes)
- Pray for Your Family Members (10 minutes)
- Pray for Your Church—Leaders, Members, Programs (5 minutes)
- Pray for Political Leaders—National, State, Local (5 minutes)
- Pray for Lost People (5 minutes)

- Pray for Your Personal Needs (5 minutes)
- Be Still and Quiet, Listening to God's Voice
  (5 minutes)

My friend, Pastor Jim Cymbala at the Brooklyn Tabernacle in Brooklyn, New York, has a prayer group in session 24/7 year-round. He tells in his book *Fresh Wind, Fresh Fire* about how the group started years ago. His people come to the designated room for their three-hour shifts of prayer at all hours. They call on the name of the Lord going through stacks of requests written on small cards by Sunday church attenders asking God to intervene in everything from employment needs to wayward children. They also pray for God's outpouring in the worship services of the church.[36] No wonder the Brooklyn Tabernacle has grown steadily for decades.

Prayer makes for a growing, holy, giving, serving, gospel-sharing, disciple-making, worshipping church. Sunday prayer, weeknight prayer, small-group prayer, individual prayer—all are good. Prayer is the key that unlocks heaven's windows. The more significant prayer becomes to your congregation, the more God will work in your midst on earth as in heaven.

Samuel Chadwick has been credited with saying, "The one concern of the devil is to keep the saints from praying. He fears nothing from prayerless studies/work/Christian activity. He laughs at our toil, mocks our wisdom, but trembles when we pray."[37]

Amen! Christians, it's time to gather with other believers and cry out to God together in prayer!

Chapter 13

PREACHING—A WORD
FROM ABOVE

Preaching has a major place in our quest for the manifest presence of God. Readers may have assumed that I think God shows up as we sing, meditate, pray, and lift our hands, but when the preacher says, "Open your Bibles, please, to Isaiah 51," the mood changes. What has been a *vertical* experience, now turns *horizontal*. The human speaker behind a pulpit begins informing the minds of his fellow human beings in the pew.

But that isn't my view at all. Preaching is the pinnacle of every worship service because it is God speaking to us. What could be more vertical than that? What God has to say to us is more important than what we have to say to Him. The dialogue that began through singing and praying now reaches its climatic point. Preaching is more than an encounter with the Word of God. It's an encounter with the God of the Word.

When I was saved as an eighteen-year-old college student, I began reading the Bible for the first time in my life. I grew up in church, but I never committed my life to Christ until I was a college freshman. At night in my dorm room, I began reading through the Gospel of John.

When I got to chapters 18–19, I paused. The Jews had prompted Jesus's arrest and brought Him before the Roman magistrate Pontius Pilate. Pilate was intrigued with this defendant from Galilee. He brought Jesus out to the seething crowd and declared, "Behold the man!" (John 19:5 KJV). When I read that famous statement for the first time, God gripped my heart. I had previously thought, in order to be a man, I needed to bench-press a certain amount of weight or knock someone down on a football field. But that night I realized that if I wanted to be a real man, I needed to live for Jesus because Jesus is the ultimate man! I prayed, "Lord Jesus, I want to be a man like You." That happened because I read my Bible, and God spoke to me. God's written Word became God's spoken Word to me. I literally heard the voice of God!

What We Want Most

That's what people are seeking. They may have heard many sermons, but in order to get through life, they need a clear, direct Word from God. They're like King Zedekiah when he was surrounded by Babylonian troops. He knew he was in trouble, so he sent for the prophet Jeremiah and asked, "Is there a word from the LORD" (Jer. 37:17)? Although Jeremiah told the king he would be captured and sent to Babylon, at least Zedekiah finally asked the right question and knew precisely where he stood with

God. I believe millions of people today are also wondering, *Is there a word from the Lord for me?*

Many years later, after a long captivity in Babylon, the Jews returned to the promised land and began rebuilding Jerusalem. They still wanted to hear from God. "And all the people gathered as one man at the square . . . *and they asked Ezra the scribe to bring the book of the law of Moses* which the LORD had given to Israel" (Neh. 8:1 NASB1995, emphasis added). They still needed to hear God's Word. Ezra didn't have to beg them to listen to his sermon; *they asked him to preach!* They were saying, "Ezra, is there a word from God? We're trying to rebuild this city before our enemies kill us. Give us a Word from heaven to hold onto!"

Ezra declared God's Word for several hours that day, "Ezra opened the book in full view of all the people, since he was elevated above everyone. As he opened it, all the people stood up" (Neh. 8:5). They wanted God's Word to be preached with clarity and conviction. That's why the people rejoiced when God spoke to them through Ezra. Today, we too face many enemies and dangers. We also need the Lord to give us a Word through preaching!

Conception and Delivery

That's why preachers must prioritize sermon preparation. Preaching is more than filling a half-hour slot on Sunday. Rather, it's discerning what God wants to say on a specific occasion and then being His mouthpiece.

In some ways, preaching a sermon is like having a baby. I heard Stephen Olford, the great expository preacher, say that a long time ago. He said that God implants a seed in the preacher's heart, a sermon idea from God's Word. The preacher then studies and prays for a period of spiritual gestation. When the message is ready, he "delivers" to the people the words God gave him. Indeed, *delivers* is a fitting term.

There are no shortcuts to genuine preaching. A preacher should never preach someone else's sermon. I believe that's stealing, plain and simple. Every preacher should avoid pre-prepared sermon outlines and preach his own sermons. I've always preached my own sermons. They may not be the best, but they're mine. I get them from God's Word through personal study.

I believe God has a warning for preachers who plagiarize other preacher's sermons in Jeremiah 23:30: "I am against the prophets . . . who steal my words from each other." God doesn't want *pirates* or *puppets* in His pulpits. He wants *prophets* who hear His Word and preach it!

If a pastor is too busy to prepare his own sermons, he's just too busy. Sermon preparation should be a top priority for every pastor. Paul commended "those who work hard at preaching and teaching" (1 Tim. 5:17). Every week a preacher should pray and seek the Lord's wisdom regarding the choice of a biblical text and then dive in and study it thoroughly. Over the years, I've found that I'll never get hold of the text until the text gets hold of my mind and soul. Only then will I be able to draw listeners close to the Father who wants to speak to all of us.

Scripture Saturated

Sermons should be based on Scripture. That main text should also be strengthened by supporting Scriptures. Every sermon should be filled with God's Word. As the preacher explains, illustrates, and applies a biblical text, what more appropriate quotations could there be than those from other texts from God's Word? The best commentary on Scripture is Scripture. That's why I pack my sermon full of Bible verses to reinforce my main text.

Scripture penetrates the heart. Hebrews 4:12 says, "For the word of God is living and effective and sharper than any double-edged sword, penetrating as far as the separation of soul and spirit, joints and marrow. It is able to judge the thoughts and intentions of the heart." Scripture goes straight to the point. Like a laser, it quickly finds the soul.

Sadly, I've heard preachers say, "Today, I'm preaching from the text," but the longer they preach, the further away *from* the text they get! They mention the Scripture text for the sermon early on, but then they engage in a plethora of stories. The vertical component of God's Word is absent. A storytelling message rests on human wisdom and becomes nothing but a sanctified speech. A real sermon is based on the inspired truth of Scripture; therefore it deserves our trust.

Contemporary illustrations have their place, so long as they don't overshadow God's Word. But I strongly encourage preachers not to spend the majority of their preaching time telling multiple stories. Illustrations should quickly and simply illuminate the biblical text in fresh, relevant ways. Good preaching based on Scripture will appeal to the heart and the mind. It will call for action and understanding, and it will move both the emotions and the intellect.

In the application portions of a sermon, I encourage the preacher to use the word *you*. Some preachers are afraid to address their listeners with "you," thinking it's too confrontational. They prefer generalizing by saying, "*We* need to be more faithful." But when Jesus preached, He used the prophetic "you." In the Sermon on the Mount, Jesus spoke directly to His listeners when He said, "But when *you* pray, go into *your* private room, shut *your* door, and pray to *your* Father who is in secret. And *your* Father who sees in secret will reward *you*" (Matt. 6:6, emphasis added). Jesus wanted them to understand He was speaking to *them*! No wonder when Jesus finished that sermon, "the crowds were astonished at his teaching, because he was teaching them like one who had authority, and not like their scribes" (Matt. 7:28–29). Perhaps all their lives they'd heard boring sermons. But Jesus was different. When He preached, He said, "I'm talking to YOU!"

Softening Up

I believe the sermon should follow a time of praise and worship. It's easier to penetrate a softened heart than a heart of stone. Many enter the sanctuary distracted or frustrated. They've endured a demanding week. The quicker they can focus on the Lord through singing and prayer the better. That way, the whole tenor of the service says, *Okay, this is about God now. It's time to forget ourselves and concentrate on Him.* After prayer and musical worship, we're ready to hear God's Word. We see that pattern in the old hymn:

> Brethren, we have met to worship
> And adore the Lord our God;
> Will you pray with all your power
> While we try to preach the Word?
> All is vain unless the Spirit
> Of the Holy One comes down;
> Brethren, pray, and holy manna
> Will be showered all around.[38]

George Atkins wrote those lyrics in 1819. He knew that worship and prayer make way for powerful preaching. Otherwise, "all is vain." Without the Spirit's anointing, nothing the preacher says is worthwhile. But when God's Spirit anoints the preaching of His Word, the congregation can feast on spiritual food shared by the preacher at the Table of the Lord.

In such a climate, preachers should not elevate and promote themselves. Pastors are the divinely chosen leaders of the church, but it's not *their* church. It's God's church. Preachers should say with John the Baptist, "He must increase, but I must decrease" (John 3:30). A preacher must not be a pulpit prima donna who enjoys the spotlight.

While I'm in this general vicinity, let me also say that no preacher should encourage his church members to call him "doctor," even if he has an earned doctorate. I've never desired for anyone to call me "Dr. Gaines," even though I have an earned PhD from a fully accredited seminary. I'd rather be called "Steve" or "Brother Steve."

That way, I can realistically admit my shortcomings. When I say, "You know, Donna and I actually get upset with each other from time to time," people relax and know I'm real. But the point is not to be cute or to build a personality attraction. Preachers should highlight the Lord and His voice. He speaks to us through the preaching of His Word, and we respond to His call.

I've heard of some congregations who engage in a second time of praise and worship following the sermon and invitation, as a response to what God said in the preacher's message. I can certainly see the value of that. When God speaks through His Word, our minds are challenged, and our hearts are stirred. That's always a great time to sing and worship the Lord.

Preaching is not meant to be a stand-alone event by any means. It is an integral component of experiencing the presence of God in the house of God. When we worship God through singing, and continue worshipping by hearing Him speak through a sermon preached by a man of God, then that word from above will help usher in the manifest presence of God.

Chapter 14

CALLING PEOPLE TO
JESUS PUBLICLY

A gulf exists in many churches between worship and evangelism. Worship, it is assumed, is what we do as Christians
on Sunday mornings (and at other times). We gather to lift up the
Lord and receive biblical teaching from His Word. Evangelism
happens outside of church—in stadiums, civic arenas, the work-
place, neighborhoods, or wherever Christians encounter those
without Jesus. Occasionally, we might use our church buildings
for evangelistic events (a musical at Christmas or Easter, for
example), when worship is secondary to evangelism. But gen-
erally speaking, "East is East and West is West, and never the
twain shall meet."[39]

The problem is, nobody told the non-Christian people who
have deep spiritual needs. Some of them wonder if God could
help them with their marriage, parenting, or that nagging sense
of guilt for the bad things they've done. They think, *I'll go to
church next Sunday morning.* After all, that's where spiritual

answers are supposed to be, right? That seems to be the easiest, least threatening thing to do. *I'll slip into the back of a church and see if it can heal the pain inside.*

Always Pursuing

We should call people to follow Jesus during a worship service. God is always planning for people to be saved. He thinks about it three hundred and sixty-five days a year, not just when we schedule our church's quarterly outreach. God is always pursuing people and calling them to Himself. As the British poet (and onetime opium addict) Francis Thompson (1859–1907) wrote in "The Hound of Heaven," God never stops pursuing lost people.

> Still with unhurrying chase,
> And unperturbed pace,
> Deliberate speed, majestic instancy,
> Came on the following Feet,
> And a Voice above their beat—
> "Naught shelters thee, who wilt not shelter Me."[40]

When was the last time somebody who knew nothing about God or Jesus Christ walked into your church service? That's actually rare. Many of the visitors in our church and yours have heard multiple sermons. The Holy Spirit has been dealing with them before they ever walked through our doors. In fact, some of them can't wait for me to give an invitation so they can receive Christ as Savior!

140

I believe the public invitation is an indispensable part of the sermon. At the end of every message, I do at least two things: 1) I ask Christians to apply the main point of my sermon to their lives, and 2) I give lost people the opportunity to be saved. That invitation to receive Christ might be the last time that person hears the gospel. I don't want to miss any opportunity. Below, I will explain in greater detail how we extend the time of invitation and response.

I've instructed our members many times that no one should leave the sanctuary at that holy moment of inviting people to Christ unless it's an absolute emergency. I then say, "Would you bow your heads with me in an attitude of prayer? If you are a Christian, in response to what I've just preached about, you need to _____" (whatever has been my sermon's theme).

Then I add, "But some of you don't know Jesus as your Savior. Let me tell you how you can be saved right now. First, you must *repent* and ask Jesus to forgive your sins. Jesus said in Luke 13:3, 'I tell you; but unless you *repent*, you will all perish as well.' *Repent* means to turn from your sin and turn to Jesus. Second, you must *believe* that Jesus died on the cross and paid the penalty for your sins and that He rose bodily from the grave and He's alive today. Jesus said in John 3:16, 'For God loved the world in this way: He gave his one and only Son, so that everyone who *believes* in him will not perish but have eternal life.' Finally, you must *receive* Jesus as your Lord and Savior by calling on His name. The Bible says, 'But to all who did *receive* him, he gave them the right to be children of God, to those who believe in his name' (John 1:12). Scripture also says, 'For everyone who *calls* on the name of the Lord will be saved' (Rom. 10:13). If you don't know Christ, you can *repent* of your sins, *believe* in Him, and *receive* Him as your Savior right now!"

Then I say, "I'd like to lead you in a prayer, just as I'd lead a young couple in their wedding vows—a phrase at a time. You can ask Christ to come into your life right where you are. Pray something like this: 'Dear Lord Jesus, . . . thank You for loving me. . . . I am a sinner. . . . I cannot save myself. . . . I repent of my sin. . . . I turn from my sin, and I turn to you. . . . Lord Jesus, I believe You died on the cross as an atoning sacrifice for my sins. . . . I believe You rose from the dead, and You're alive. . . . I repent, and I believe. Now I receive You. . . . I call on your name. . . . Save me right now, Lord Jesus. . . . Wash me and cleanse me with Your blood. . . . Fill me with Your Spirit . . . and help me to live for You for the rest of my life. . . . In Jesus's holy name, amen!'"

Then I say, "If you just prayed to receive Christ, heaven is rejoicing right now, and we'd like to rejoice with you as well (the congregation often applauds). We're about to sing our final worship song. When we start singing, I invite you to come to the front of the sanctuary to meet one of our counselors. Tell them you've prayed to receive Christ or that you'd like to do that now. They'll rejoice with you, pray with you, and give you some materials to help grow in Christ. And if you need a Bible, we will give you one."

"If you are a Christian but you've never been baptized, come and set up a time to be baptized. Every person in the New Testament who believed savingly in Jesus was baptized. Baptism doesn't save you. It just shows that you are saved. It's a picture of dying to your old life of sin, being buried in Christ, and being raised to walk in newness of life. Baptism is the first way you tell the world you belong to Jesus. It's like putting on a wedding ring. The ring doesn't make you married; it just shows that you are married. Baptism doesn't save you, but it does show that you are saved. Come and set up a time for your baptism today. Perhaps the Lord is leading you to make Bellevue your church home. Come and talk with someone here today. Or maybe you sense that the Lord might be calling you to preach the gospel or to serve in some other form of vocational, ministerial service. If so, I invite all of you to whom God is speaking to come today. Please come now as we sing."

This part of the worship service is not rushed. It takes five to ten minutes. That's okay. God is working in people's hearts.

Theirs to Decide

Again, at the end of every service, I invite people to come and: 1) be saved by asking Christ to be their Lord and Savior, 2) set up a time to be baptized if they've already received Christ, 3) start the process of joining our fellowship, 4) ask for prayer, and 5) ask to be anointed with oil and prayed over for healing. That's just part of the rhythm of our fellowship.

Some preachers might be thinking: *But what if I preach my heart out, and nobody responds at the invitation?* That's not a failure on the preacher's part, provided he has made the message clear. It's not my job to produce numerical results. It's my job to make the offer of Christ available. The Holy Spirit does the rest in His timing. He doesn't need me to make people feel guilty. He only wants me to politely and warmly explain what they need to do to make a decision. When I do that, they must act on their own.

Peter concluded his sermon on the day of Pentecost in this manner: "With many other words he testified and strongly urged them, saying, 'Be saved from this corrupt generation!'" (Acts 2:40). The Greek word for "strongly urged" here is *parakaleo*, literally, "to call for." Peter gave an invitation and "about three thousand people were added to them" (v. 41). It was like a Billy Graham crusade! The audience didn't just listen and walk away; they made public commitments to follow Christ.

For people who are too timid to step out in front of a large crowd, I say at the end, "We're about to conclude this service, but God's invitation isn't over. If you still need to be saved, baptized, join the church, or pray with someone, our counselors will be here at the front to meet you after the service. Please don't leave here without Jesus." People respond to this "P.S." almost every week.

People don't have to walk a church aisle to be saved. But I believe a public profession of faith is healthy and biblical. Whenever the late Billy Graham preached in his crusades, he always called people who were receiving Christ as Savior to do it publicly. Graham noted that every time Jesus called someone to follow Him, He called them publicly. Jesus has no incognito followers.

If the main reason we come to church is to meet with God, we should extend that privilege to everyone. That said, I don't aim most of my sermons exclusively to the unsaved. Probably 95 percent of my sermons are geared primarily toward Christians. But even then, God's Word can speak to lost people. God says this about His Word: "So my word that comes from my mouth will not return to me empty, but it will accomplish what I please and will prosper in what I send it to do" (Isa. 55:11). Years ago, I heard someone say that God's Word is a two-edged sword—it comforts the afflicted and afflicts the comfortable. We need both to happen in our churches.

God at Work

Whenever our counselors first meet a person responding to the invitation, they ask: "What's your name and what is your decision?" They don't waste time on peripherals—where the person lives, what their occupation is, and so forth. They get right to the point.

I'll never forget a Sunday morning when I personally counseled a woman during the invitation time. She cried as I asked her with a quiet voice, "What is your decision?" She then blurted out through her tears, "I want it all!" I was bumfuzzled and said, "You 'want it all'? I don't understand." "All that stuff you just talked about!" she said. "I want to be saved, baptized, and join the church—I want it all! The whole works!"

She came seeking the Lord with all her heart and desired to be a fully devoted, obedient child of God. The Holy Spirit had touched that woman deeply. Half measures weren't good enough. One of our counselors sat with her and led her to find "it all" in a new life in Christ!

She responded publicly because we invited her to come to Jesus publicly. This kind of encounter with God is as important as any worship chorus we sing or any prayer we pray. When Jesus penetrates the human heart and draws people to Himself, we know He's at work among us.

Oh, for more preachers, Christians, and churches who unashamedly call lost people to Jesus publicly!

Chapter 15

FIVE ENEMIES OF REVIVAL

We've spent a decent about of time discussing how to proactively prepare the way for receiving God's rivers of living water in revival. Now we must look at several sinister forces that are capable of quenching the momentum of spiritual awakening. These dark forces can thwart God's heavenly waters from flowing as freely as they should. They stall and stunt the work of God. Like intruders, they short-circuit the power of spiritual awakening. There are at least five "enemies" of revival: traditionalism, formalism, fanaticism, liberalism, and legalism. Any one of these, or any combination of these, can strangle, stifle, and even stop revival.

The apostle Paul spoke about "enemies" of the gospel and the church: "For I have often told you, and now say again with tears, that many live as *enemies of the cross of Christ*" (Phil. 3:18, emphasis added). Jesus and His followers have always had enemies, and so do spiritual awakening and revival.

The Enemy of Traditionalism

The Jewish Pharisees were religious traditionalists. They studied and revered their religious traditions more than they did the Scriptures. They actually blurred Scripture with their religious traditions. That's why the Pharisees got angry when Jesus's disciples failed to ceremonially wash their hands before they ate a meal. In Matthew 15:2, they asked Jesus, "Why do your disciples break the tradition of the elders? For they don't wash their hands when they eat." Jesus responded with an even better question: "Why do you break God's commandment because of your tradition?" (v. 3). Then Jesus reminded them that they frequently broke the fifth commandment ("Honor your father and mother") by refusing to financially help their aging parents by claiming that they'd already dedicated all their money to God. Jesus said, "In this way, you have nullified the word of God because of your tradition" (v. 6). When you elevate human traditions above God's Word, you embrace an enemy of revival—traditionalism.

Here are some classic cries of traditionalism I've heard:

- "That may be the way the early church did it, but we don't do that here."
- "In our church, men wear coats and ties, and women wear dresses."
- "We don't clap our hands or lift our hands in a worship service."

- "We don't like drums or guitars; we prefer a piano and an organ."
- "Women should never pray or be an usher in a worship service."

Question: Where is any of that addressed in the Bible? Jesus rebuked the Pharisees for having this kind of attitude. *Tradition* itself isn't bad as long as it's in line with Scripture. But *traditionalism*—i.e., doing things in church just because that's the way your father and grandfather always did it—is an enemy to the church. Listen again to Jesus's rebuke to all religious traditionalists: "This people honors me with their lips, but their heart is far from me. They worship me in vain, teaching as doctrines human commands" (Matt. 15:8–9).

Traditionalism is an enemy of revival.

The Enemy of Formalism

Similar to traditionalism, formalism is when God's people are more concerned with religious procedure and protocol than with loving God and people. Jesus denounced the scribes and Pharisees of His day because they loved the "show of formalism,"

> "They love the place of honor at banquets, the front seats in the synagogues, greetings in the marketplaces, and to be called 'Rabbi' by people.

"But you are not to be called 'Rabbi,' because you have one Teacher, and you are all brothers and sisters. Do not call anyone on earth your father, because you have one Father, who is in heaven. You are not to be called instructors either, because you have one Instructor, the Messiah. The greatest among you will be your servant. Whoever exalts himself will be humbled, and whoever humbles himself will be exalted." (Matt. 23:6–12)

Jesus said that these people with selfish egos loved their religious formalism and privileges. He then warned His disciples not to imitate them. A contemporary paraphrase of the Matthew 23 instruction above might read something like, "Don't be called rabbi—I'm your teacher; you're all brothers. Don't call any religious person father—God alone is your spiritual Father. And don't be called leaders—I'm your Leader. If you want to achieve greatness, be a servant. If you exalt yourself, I will humble you. But if you humble yourself, I will exalt you."

Religious formalism desires dignity over deity. It prefers being "proper" over experiencing God's power and presence. In the Old Testament, when God poured out His Spirit on seventy elders who assisted Moses in judging God's people, Joshua got upset: "Joshua son of Nun, assistant to Moses since his youth, responded, 'Moses, my lord, stop them!' But Moses asked him, 'Are you jealous on my account? If only all the LORD's people were prophets and the LORD would place his Spirit on them!'

Then Moses returned to the camp along with the elders of Israel" (Num. 11:28–30).

For a moment, Joshua was guilty of religious formalism. He only wanted his mentor (Moses) to prophesy. But Moses knew God had shared the spiritual gift of prophecy with others.

For the religious formalist, church is a production. It's a scripted program—a show for man, not worship for God. Religious formalists love it when choirs pompously "file in" the correct way, at the right time, wearing the right robe. Formalists say music must be classical, not contemporary. Religious formalists allow short, nonconfrontational sermonettes that never challenge sinners with God's truth. Religious formalists loath it when congregants audibly respond, "Amen! Hallelujah! Praise the Lord!" They despise lifting holy hands and clapping joyful hands to God. They see no place for weeping and praying at the altar. And they don't believe in praying for the sick, anointing them with oil, and asking God to heal them.

For the formalist, the platform is a stage, the preacher and singers are actors and actresses, and the congregation is the audience. But that's not what God desires in a worship service. In a genuine worship service, there's no man-exalting formality! There's just heartfelt worship offered up humbly to the Lord by everyone. The only "audience" is God Himself! True Christians worship for God's glory, not their own! They understand 1 Samuel 16:7: "Humans do not see what the LORD sees, for humans see what is visible, but the LORD sees the heart."

Formalism is and always has been a sinister enemy of revival and spiritual awakening.

The Enemy of Fanaticism

Religious fanaticism is when worshippers go beyond Scripture and emphasize experience an emotionalism over the Word of God. Consider it a polar opposite error to formalism. Paul dealt with fanaticism with the church at Corinth in 1 Corinthians 14. Some of the Corinthian Christians were abusing their spiritual freedom when the church gathered to worship the Lord. Paul instructed them by telling them they were right to engage in the usage of spiritual gifts in their gatherings as a church, but they needed to do it in an orderly manner. Paul said that while tongues is a legitimate gift, it is a lesser gift. He stressed whoever prophesied was greater than one who spoke in tongues because the one who prophesies edifies and strengthens others (vv. 3–5).

Paul also spoke against the chaos that some of the Corinthians were causing in their worship services. He gave the example that when warriors go to battle, a bugler makes a battle-cry sound that the army recognizes so they can fight victoriously. Likewise, when Christians gathered together in church, they needed to primarily speak in their common, earthly languages so everyone could understand. If they spoke out loud in tongues in a worship service, they wouldn't edify the others because they wouldn't be able to understand them (vv. 6–9).

Paul stressed that they shouldn't just think about what was best for them, but they were to edify and build up other Christians (vv. 10–12). That's exactly what Paul did. Paul gave up his "rights" in a public worship service out of his love for other Christians. He didn't want to be a stumbling block. Paul spoke and prayed in tongues, but he preferred not to do it publicly in a service (vv. 13–19) because he didn't want God's house to be a house of confusion (v. 33). Paul wanted God's house to be a house of peace and edification.

Fanaticism tries to worship God in selfish, fleshly, unbiblical ways. There's nothing wrong with emotions. God's greatest commandment is to love God with all your heart, soul, mind, and strength (cf. Mark 12:30). You should worship God emotionally with 100 percent of your heart and soul, but you should also avoid engaging in emotional fanaticism by seeking the sensation for the sake of the sensation. Jesus warned about that when He said, "An evil and adulterous generation demands a sign" (Matt. 16:4).

In the First Great Awakening (mid-1700s), there were cases of religious fanaticism. When John Wesley preached in England at Bristol and at Kensington, a few people fell down, screamed, growled, and barked, and their bodies writhed in physical contortions. Some of them did those things just to imitate others and to give the impression that they were "spiritual."

In our day I've heard of excessive, fanatical happenings such as people claiming that gold dust appeared in the palms of their hands, angel feathers were lying on the church altar, and that the Lord was causing them to laugh uncontrollably. I don't see any of those things in Scripture. Those instances seem to be indicative of religious fanaticism, which is an enemy of real revival. God wants to send revival fire, but the enemy wants us to pursue spiritual wildfires and distractions.

Fanaticism is an ugly enemy of revival and spiritual awakening.

The Enemy of Liberalism

The first-century Jewish Sadducees were religious liberals. They didn't believe in resurrection after death (cf. Luke 20:27), or angels and spirits (cf. Acts 23:8), even though all of these are scriptural. Liberalism denies the authority and accuracy of Scripture. If the Bible were a highway, liberalism would be the "ditch on the left." Liberalism takes away from Scripture by questioning it and denying it. That's precisely what Satan did when he tempted Eve in the garden of Eden.

> Now the serpent was the most cunning of all the wild animals that the LORD God had made. He said to the woman, "Did God really say, 'You can't eat from any tree in the garden'?"
>
> The woman said to the serpent, "We may eat the fruit from the trees in the garden. But about the fruit of the tree in the middle of the garden, God said, 'You must not eat it or touch it, or you will die.'"
>
> "No! You will certainly not die," the serpent said to the woman. "In fact, God knows that when you eat it your eyes will be opened and you will be like God, knowing good and evil."
> (Gen. 3:1–5)

Liberalism denies the authority and accuracy of Scripture. It says, "God is love. He will give salvation to everyone. There is no hell." To those living sinful lifestyles, liberalism says, "Neither do

I condemn you," but it refuses to also say, "Go and sin no more!" It tries to lift up those who've fallen into sin without lifting up the standard of God's Word. Liberalism says, "The Bible *contains* God's Word, but IT is NOT God's Word." Liberalism says, "Some of the Bible is inspired but not ALL of it."

But the Bible itself says that every word of Scripture is inspired by God. The psalmist affirmed this when he said, "*The entirety of your word is truth*, each of your righteous judgments endures forever" (Ps. 119:160, emphasis added). Likewise, Jesus prayed to God the Father and said, "Sanctify them by the truth; *your word is truth*" (John 17:17, emphasis added). And Paul said to Timothy, "*All Scripture* is inspired by God" (2 Tim. 3:16, emphasis added).

Liberalism says that Jesus is one way to God but not the only way. But Jesus said He was, is, and always will be the only way to God. No one can come to God unless they come through Jesus Christ (cf. John 14:6; Acts 4:12; 1 Tim. 2:5). Liberalism says that heaven is real but hell is not. Liberalism says that all people will go to heaven and no one will go to hell. But Jesus said that hell is real and whoever doesn't repent and believe in Him will spend eternity there (cf. Luke 13:3).

Liberalism says that marriage is between any two people in love, which includes homosexuals and lesbians. But the Bible and Jesus Himself both say that biblical marriage is exclusively heterosexual and monogamous—one man and one woman (cf. Gen. 2:24; Matt. 19:4–5). Liberalism says that abortion is "health care" or even a right in the name of a woman having control over her own body, but it disregards the rights of the other body involved in an abortion—the body of the baby. The Bible confirms unborn babies are living human beings—"For it was you who created my inward parts; you knit me together in my mother's womb. I will praise you because I have been remarkably and wondrously made" (Ps. 139:13–14).

Liberalism picks and chooses what it likes from what Scripture says, making humans the authority instead of God. It is and always has been an enemy of revival and spiritual awakening.

The Enemy of Legalism

The early Christians faced the danger of religious legalism. When Paul and Barnabas went on their missionary journeys, they shared the gospel with many Jews and Gentiles. But when they shared the gospel with Gentiles, none of them were forced to adhere to Jewish religious traditions before they became Christians. Gentile men were not required to be circumcised, nor were they forced to obey the Old Testament Law, before they could be converted. They became believers by repenting of sin and placing their faith in Christ.

But soon, some of the Pharisees who'd converted to Christianity in Jerusalem began teaching that Gentiles also needed to be circumcised and obey the law in order to be saved. That is, before a Gentile could convert to Christ, he had first to convert to Judaism. Paul and Barnabas categorically rejected that idea (cf. Acts 15:1–2). By the end of Acts 15, the church at Jerusalem decided that Gentiles did not have to adhere to Jewish customs to become Christians. They simply needed to repent and place their faith in Jesus Christ.

If the Bible is a highway, legalism is the "ditch on the right." It's the opposite "ditch" of liberalism on the "left." Legalism turns Christianity into a list of man-made rules instead of a love relationship with God in Christ. Out of all these enemies of revival, legalism is often the meanest. Legalists demand keeping the rules, but they can often be excessively mean to other people. Legalism says to the sinner, "Go and sin no more," but it refuses to also say, "Neither do I condemn you." Legalism lifts up God's standard in Scripture but fails to lift up the sinner who has fallen. Legalism shouts: "Don't sin," but offers little hope to the fallen. Legalists often disguise themselves as "conservatives." Theologically, I am to the right and conservative. I also lean to the right regarding political issues like abortion and marriage (which in my mind are ethical issues). I'm to the right theologically and politically. But I don't want to be to the right of Scripture!

Legalism is often more dangerous than liberalism. If liberalism has slain its thousands, legalism has slain its tens of thousands. If liberalism is love without law, legalism is law without love. The fact is, you need both love and law to be biblically balanced.

The legalistic Pharisees had Jesus crucified. Indeed, legalism has always been an enemy of revival. It steals, kills, and destroys.

Conclusion

There are at least five archenemies of revival. Any one of these—traditionalism, formalism, fanaticism, liberalism, or legalism—can keep you and your church from experiencing genuine spiritual awakening. All five are demonic strongholds that must be eliminated by repentance, prayer, and fasting and by living daily in God's Word and in the fullness of His Spirit.

Are you guilty of any of these five ungodly enemies of revival? If so, repent and ask the Lord to forgive you.

Chapter 16

DISCONTENTED BUT HOPEFUL

Two words in the English language are close to each other in meaning. One is considered to be negative while the other is considered to be positive. It's considered a bad thing to be *complacent*, but it's a good thing to be *content*. The first word carries the connotation of being sleepy, lethargic, and not paying attention to important issues. The latter implies coming to terms with the way things really are. Spiritually speaking, I'm not sure I want to be either.

Late in his life, writing from a Roman prison cell, the apostle Paul told the Philippian Christians, "I don't say this out of need, for I have learned to be content in whatever circumstances I find myself. I know how to make do with little, and I know how to make do with a lot. In any and all circumstances I have learned the secret of being content—whether well fed or hungry, whether in abundance or in need. I am able to do all things through him who strengthens me. Still, you did well by partnering with me in my hardship" (Phil. 4:11–14).

Paul said he had "learned the secret of being content," even in the midst of persecution.

Yet, in the previous chapter, the apostle, who was well into his fifties or sixties, aspired passionately to know Christ in a deeper, more mature and fulfilling way. He said, "Not that I have already reached the goal or am already perfect, but I make every effort to take hold of it because I also have been taken hold of by Christ Jesus. Brothers and sisters, I do not consider myself to have taken hold of it. But one thing I do: Forgetting what is behind and reaching forward to what is ahead, I pursue as my goal the prize promised by God's heavenly call in Christ Jesus" (Phil. 3:12–14).

A close analysis of these two texts, written to the same recipients (the Philippians), shows that Paul was *content materially* but *discontented spiritually*. Paul did not crave material possessions. He faithfully followed Jesus, who also rejected materialism and said, "Foxes have dens, and birds of the sky have nests, but the Son of Man has no place to lay his head" (Matt. 8:20). On the physical plane, Paul (like Jesus) traveled light. He wasn't attached to worldly creature comforts. But spiritually, Paul abounded in heavenly riches.

Too many Christians today are the opposite. They are *content spiritually* and *discontented materially*. Their walk with the Lord rocks along comfortably with just a minimal investment of time and energy. Meanwhile, they feel a need to trade up to a bigger house, a newer car, and plan ever more exclusive vacations. They often violate the tenth commandment because they covet what others have that they don't possess.

As a follower of Jesus, pursuing the American dream is a dangerous way to live. The *Rocky III* movie has a poignant scene where Mickey Goldmill, Rocky's longtime trainer, says to the now successful and somewhat lethargic champion, "Three years ago, you were supernatural. You were hard and you were nasty. You had this cast-iron jaw. But then, the worst thing happened to you that could happen to a fighter. You got civilized." Mickey was telling Rocky that he wasn't hungry enough to win against a real opponent. He'd lost "the eye of the tiger."

That also happens to pastors and church members. We start out in our walk with Christ with hearts of holy blaze. Our prayers are energizing, Scripture intake is rewarding, Christian fellowship is edifying, and sharing the gospel verbally with lost people is as good as it gets! Everything seems so dynamic and new. It's like the first days of love early in a marriage.

But then somewhere along the way we settle down into a religious routine and start going through the motions. We learn how to act spiritual, how to do church, and how to maintain a religious façade. We move forward on spiritual autopilot. Everything looks good to observers, but deep inside, we know we've lost something we used to have.

When I first met Christ in college, all I wanted to do was listen to Christian music, worship the Lord, witness, pray, go to church, fellowship with other believers, and read the Bible. Over four decades later, what haunts me today is whether or not that same passion is alive and well in my life. Yes, my walk with the Lord has matured. I have a greater theological understanding and background. But deep inside I sometimes wonder as time moves on if I've lost something spiritually that I once had. Do I still have that deep hunger for the Lord Jesus and His presence, or have I become *content* in an unhealthy way?

What about our churches? Are we content to have just a few more people in the pews this year than last? If our church's budget income increases 5 percent, is that "success"? Our culture is becoming increasingly corrupt and carnal every year. How can we be content to settle for a sliver of growth? How can we not long for the glory of God to once again fill the house of God?

Return to the Original

Discontentment can be a blessing when it's combined with a hopeful attitude. The spiritual discontentment we experience today is not with God. It's with us. God hasn't changed, but many Christians have. We're not as hungry, obedient, or committed as we should be. Too often, the church looks more like the world around us and not enough like the church in the book of Acts. The apostle Peter said, "I urge you as *strangers and exiles* to abstain from sinful desires that wage war against the soul" (1 Pet. 2:11, emphasis added). Christians aren't supposed to be like the world. We're to be delightfully different. We're Christ's soldiers who are camping behind enemy lines. We're "pilgrims passing through" this wicked world on our way to heaven. We should never feel comfortable down here.

Allow me to admit the obvious: much of what we're doing in our churches today isn't working. Remember that the rhetorical definition of *insanity* is *continuing to do the same thing over and over again while expecting different results.* If short sermons, skillful songs, and pretty church programs could save America, our nation would have shown evidence of mass revival and cultural healing. We need an outpouring of divine power. We need the Lord Himself to show up in our churches in grace and glory. The church today must not be content until we look like the church in the book of Acts.

Hopeful Surprises in Unlikely Places

When God shows up in a church, people will do whatever it takes to get there, even if it's in the wilderness like the area where John the Baptist preached. Location doesn't really matter. People will be spiritually drawn to the glory of God in the house of God.

I can think of at least two examples in my own experience over the years that make me hopeful for the future of Christianity in America.

Years ago, my wife and I took our children on a two-week vacation to New England. We visited Williamsburg, Washington, D.C., Philadelphia, Boston, New York City, and Plymouth Rock. During our time in New York City, we saw the Broadway musical *Beauty and the Beast*, Central Park, the Empire State Building, and other great sights. On Sunday, we went to the Brooklyn Tabernacle Church. We'd listened to the music of their Grammy Award-winning choir for years, and we wanted to see and hear it in person.

We arrived an hour early for the noon service, only to find ourselves joining a long line of people waiting to get inside the

1,500-seat building. I looked at the crowd that was waiting and walked to the front of the line to discuss the situation with the doorkeeper. I asked him if the choir sang in that service, and he said, "No, the noon service features the student choir. Our adult choir will sing later in the 3:30 service and the 7:30 service. But you'll need to arrive early to get into either of those services as well."

As I talked with him, I learned that he was an ex-cocaine addict from New Jersey whose life had been radically changed through the ministry of the Brooklyn Tabernacle. After he came to faith in the Lord Jesus, he moved from New Jersey to Brooklyn so he could serve as an usher there and sing in the choir.

So, with extra time on our hands, our family caught a cab to the World Trade Center. We took our children to the top of that building (an experience no longer available since its destruction on September 11, 2001). We arrived back at the Brooklyn Tabernacle around 2:30. As the choir was warming up, we sat and bathed our souls in their music. Even their practices were Spirit anointed! They didn't wear robes, but they sang with gusto from their hearts. We looked around at the crowd as it was gathering and saw an eclectic congregation: African Americans, whites, Latinos, Asians, rich and poor. You couldn't help but feel welcome there.

The worship service began, and we were immediately swept up in an awesome atmosphere of praise. The choir's music was incredible. Even the announcements in this church were a blessing. For example, they announced a special time that week for parents to bring their school-age children for prayer for the upcoming school year. "Would you like us to pray over your children for safety as they head back to the classroom? If so, bring them." In such a high-crime area of the city, I could tell this was a definite concern.

Pastor Jim Cymbala preached an excellent, biblical, Christ-focused sermon. At the end of his message, he called for people to respond. He invited people who wanted to be saved to come and meet with counselors, and he asked people who wanted to be prayed for to come as well. I immediately stepped forward and went to the altar. I met with a man and prayed with him. Afterward, I asked him if there was any way I could be prayed over by Pastor Jim. I told him I was a pastor too, and I was hoping he'd be willing to do that. In a minute or so, Brother Jim came over and greeted me. He was tired after preaching for the third time that day, but he laid hands on me and prayed for me for several minutes asking God to bless my ministry. It was a sweet time of prayer that I will never forget. If it hadn't been for our young children running out of steam, we would have stayed for the next worship service. THE PRESENCE OF GOD WAS IN THAT PLACE! They weren't Baptists like us, but God was moving there. We headed back to our hotel in Manhattan feeling loved and blessed.

The church building had been congested, the streets were noisy, the church literally had *zero* parking places, yet they were and still are reaching people by the thousands in a spiritually dark region. Pastor Cymbala once told me, "Sometimes I think we are the most seeker-*UN*friendly church in America." Yet the presence of the Lord seems to override all of that.

Since I've been at Bellevue, Jim Cymbala and I have become good friends. He has preached regularly for us at our annual Awesome August services. Some of his singers have joined him when he comes. He has also allowed me to preach at the Brooklyn Tabernacle several times. He's a like-minded brother in Christ. We both share a deep desire and hopefulness for God's manifest presence to saturate us, our family members, our churches, and other churches as well.

A few years after I first worshipped at the Brooklyn Tabernacle, I also experienced the manifest presence of God in a rural church. I'd been invited to preach at Bethlehem Baptist Church in (are you ready for the name of the community?) Lickskillet, Alabama. It took us awhile to find the church. When we finally arrived, it looked like no one was there. I was wondering, *Why in the world did I accept this invitation and drive all this way to preach to empty seats?* Then I saw a man and asked him if I was at the right place. He said, "Yes, you're at the right location, just the wrong building. The service tonight will be back there in our gym." I thought, *The gym?*

I walked back to the gym, opened the door, and there were several hundred enthusiastic people getting ready to worship the Lord! The singers and the band were practicing and had a down-home sound like the country group Brooks and Dunn. In fact, the lead singer that night sounded a lot like Ronnie Dunn. I found out they had over seven hundred that morning in worship, and they were packed again that night! Their buildings didn't resemble the Brooklyn Tabernacle, but they had the same sweet sense of the presence of the Lord.

The pastor had been an evangelist before becoming pastor of that church. He had a joyful spirit, and he led the worship service in a Spirit-filled manner. Before long, he introduced a woman named Clair, who'd been playing guitar with the praise band. He asked her to sing a song. The moment she said her first sentence in her introduction, it rang a bell. *I know that voice!* I told myself. I stood up in the middle of her introduction and shouted, "Clair? Are you Clair Lynch?" The Claire Lynch I referred to had won Grammy awards for her bluegrass music. She said, "Yes, I am." Then I shouted back, "Could I play guitar and sing a song or two with you?" She agreed while everyone applauded. I went up to the platform, borrowed a guitar, and sang a few hymns with *the* Clair Lynch. When I sat down, we sang more songs, I preached, gave a gospel invitation, and several people received Jesus as Lord and Savior. The presence of God was all over that place—right there in Lickskillet, Alabama!

I came back to Bethlehem Baptist Church a year later and preached again. The church was even larger. People from all around the area drove many miles every week to attend that church because the Lord's presence was all over their ministry. It reminded me of something Dr. Jerry Falwell once told me. He said, "I'd rather drive across town and be fed than walk across the street and be fooled." Amen! If the Lord is in the house, it's definitely worth the drive!

At the end of the day, the most important things about a church aren't its location or its outward appearance. Looks can be deceiving. The lawn may be immaculately groomed, and the building may be architecturally amazing, but without the anointing and presence of the Holy Spirit, all of that is meaningless. On the other hand, the address may be hard to find, the carpet may be worn, the steeple may be crooked (or even missing), but if Jesus is exalted and the Spirit of God is present, great things will happen. The Lord's presence is what gives us hope!

What Does Jesus See in Us?

When the One whose eyes are like fire wrote to the church at Ephesus (Rev. 2:1–7), He looked past the externals to the heart of their congregation. They had a great heritage. They had been one of Paul's favorite churches. Jesus Himself complemented them, saying they had persevered through hardships. Yet they were in danger of losing the oil that supplied their lampstand. Why? Jesus said, "I have this against you: You have abandoned the love you had at first" (Rev. 2:4).

Oil is used in the New Testament as a metaphor for the Holy Spirit. A church without oil for its lampstand is a liability to God. Without fuel to light the way, it might as well be shuttered. Jesus knows what's going on in my church and in yours. He walks through every room, office, corridor, and parking lot. He knows what's said in every class, committee meeting, counseling session, and casual conversation. Dare we brag to one another when He is listening?

Is there a spirit of prayer and humility or a spirit of pride and arrogance in your church? Is their consistency or hypocrisy? Is there genuine love or pretense? He knows the choir and orchestra.

Do they sing for Jesus or to be heard by the congregation? Do they rejoice when someone else gets the solo, or are they jealous?

He knows every teacher of the church. Do they teach to glorify God by bringing lost people to Christ? Do they disciple believers to build them up in the Lord or to build up their own reputation as a "faithful disciple maker"? As church members, are they under pastoral authority, or do they have an independent spirit and desire to do their own thing?

Jesus knows every church and every church member. He's aware of whether you come to church to be seen by others or to meet with Him. Do you tithe and give offerings to the church for a tax break? What if our government stops allowing church contributions to be tax-deductible? That's how it is in most countries in the world. Will you still obey the Lord and give at least 10 percent of your income to His church? And what about missions? Do you go on a mission trip thousands of miles away from your home to share the gospel with people in other countries but rarely (if ever) share the gospel with anyone in your neighborhood? Do you say you love other Christians but tear them down in gossip behind their backs? Do you look at porn online on Saturday night and go to church on Sunday and say, "Praise the Lord"?

Jesus knows all about you and me. He tells us just as He told the Ephesian church, "I have this against you: You have abandoned the love you had at first" (Rev. 2:4). We can choose to be a *committed* Christian or a *convenient* Christian. I'm hopeful that we will be as committed as the Christians in the book of Acts who sometimes surrendered their lives for Christ.

At the beginning of this book, I shared a statement from J. B. Phillips. Here's how he concluded the preface of his translation of the book of Acts:

> Of course it is easy to "write off" this little history of the church's first beginnings as simply an account of an enthusiastic but ill regulated and unorganized adolescence, to be followed by a well-disciplined maturity in which embarrassing irregularities no longer appear. But that is surely too easy an explanation all together. We in the modern church have unquestionably lost something. Whether it is due to the atrophy of the quality which the New Testament calls "faith," whether it is due to a stifling churchiness, whether it is due to our sinful complacency over the scandal of a divided Church, or whatever the cause may be, very little of the modern Church could bear comparison with the spiritual drive, the genuine fellowship, and the . . . unconquerable courage of the Young Church.[41]

No Time to Hesitate

I pray daily that the Lord will allow me to live long enough to see a revival, another invasion of God's presence in our churches and in individual Christians. I am hopeful that I will! For that to happen, we must go wholeheartedly after the Lord and plead with Him to send showers of blessings. We need to get off the fence and go full speed after our great God.

When we lived in Alabama, I drove our children to school every morning. One morning as we were headed toward our children's schools, a little squirrel ran out in the road ahead of us. He got right in the middle of the road, saw me heading his way, and froze. He didn't know whether to keep running to the other side or to go back to where he'd started. He looked both ways several times while he stood still in his position. My girls screamed, "Daddy, don't kill the squirrel!" I slammed on the breaks, and my truck stopped two feet short of that lucky ball of fur. As soon as I stopped, he darted across to the other side, jumped onto a tree, and shot to the top.

I've known some Christians who remind me of that little squirrel. They toy with the idea of following Jesus wholeheartedly. But when they get in the middle of their walk with the Lord, they see something threatening headed their way, and they freeze spiritually. They don't know whether to press on and keep following Jesus or to turn around and run back the way they came.

Friends, it's time for Christians and churches to go one way or the other. You can't walk with the Lord Jesus and live in fear like a squirrel in the middle of the road. Christians who live in fear go back and forth in life and accomplish little for the Lord. But He is more than ready and able to help you overcome all your fears so you can walk in faith.

Brothers and sisters, it's time to run across the road, get to the other side, and press into the manifest presence of God! It's time to be all-in, living daily in His glorious presence.

Christians in America haven't seen a nationwide revival since the late 1960s and early 1970s. The tide of revival has been "out" for decades. I think it's been out long enough.

Will you join me today? Let's pray, fast, repent, stay filled with the Holy Spirit, and be completely available to the Lord. Let's plead with God and ask Him to send His heavenly fire upon our churches, our denominations, our preachers, and our nation once again!

I am hopeful because I believe God wants all of that to happen. I am hopeful because I believe more and more Christians desire revival. I'm hopeful and I'm fervently praying.

I'm discontented but hopeful. I believe *it's time for God to come back to church!*

ABOUT THE AUTHOR

Dr. Steve Gaines has been the senior pastor at Bellevue Baptist Church in Memphis, Tennessee, since 2005. He earned his bachelor of science (BS, 1979) at Union University in Jackson, Tennessee, and his master of divinity (MDiv, 1984) and doctor of philosophy (PhD, 1991) at Southwestern Baptist Theological Seminary in Ft. Worth, Texas. Since 1983, Steve has pastored churches in Texas, Tennessee, and Alabama, before coming to Bellevue. His primary focus in ministry is prayer and preaching. He served as the president of the Southern Baptist Convention (2016–2018) and has also served in other denominational positions over the years, in addition to preaching for many denominational events at national, state, and local levels. Steve has been married to Donna since 1980. They have four married children and eighteen grandchildren.

NOTES

1. J. B. Phillips, *The Young Church in Action* (New York: Macmillan, 1955), vii. This paraphrase later became part of Phillips's *The New Testament in Modern English*, but the Acts preface was not included in the larger work.

2. "Battle Belongs," written by Brian Johnson and Phil Wickham, © 2020 Simply Global Songs (BMI) / Phil Wickham Music (BMI) (admin at EssentialMusicPublishing.com). All rights reserved. Used by permission.

3. "Same God," written by Chris Brown, Steven Furtick, Patrick Barrett, and Brandon Lake, © 2022 Music by Elevation Worship Publishing (BMI) (admin at EssentialMusicPublishing.com). All rights reserved. Used by permission.

4. I will comment more on what I mean by fanaticism in chapter 15.

5. Matt Redman, *The Unquenchable Worshipper: Coming Back to the Heart of Worship* (Grand Rapids: Baker, 2001). Posted on https://deanmerrill.com/did-the-upper-room-have-an-ipod-player, accessed October 26, 2023. Song lyrics © 1999 Kingsway's Thankyou Music.

6. C. H. Spurgeon, *The Soul-Winner: How to Lead Sinners to the Saviour* (Grand Rapids: William B. Eerdmans, 1963), 106–7.

7. Richard L. Bushman, *The Great Awakening: Documents on the Revival of Religion, 1740–1745* (Chapel Hill, NC: University of North Carolina Press, 1970), 4.

8. George Whitefield, *George Whitefield's Journals* (London: The Banner of Truth Trust, 1960), 352.

9. Ralph G. Turnbull, *A History of Preaching*, vol. 3 (Grand Rapids, MI: Baker Book House, 1974) 67.

10. Peter F. Gunther, ed., *Sermon Classics by Great Preachers* (Chicago: Moody Press, 1982), 19–20.

11. Arnold Dallimore, *George Whitefield*, vol. 1 (Edinburgh: The Banner of Truth Trust, originally published in 1970; reprinted in 2001), 427.

12. Mark A. Noll, *A History of Christianity in the United States and Canada* (Grand Rapids: William B. Eerdmans, 1992), 91.

13. Noll, *A History of Christianity in the United States and Canada*, 166.

14. Benjamin Rice Lacy, *Revivals in the Midst of the Years* (Hopewell, VA: Royal Publishers, 1968), 70.

15. Chauncey A. Goodrich, "Narrative of Revivals of Religion in Yale College," *American Quarterly Register* 10 (Feb. 1838): 295–96.

16. Noll, *History of Christianity in the United States and Canada*, 169.

17. Noll, *History of Christianity in the United States and Canada*, 167.

18. L. C. Rudolph, *Frances Asbury* (Nashville: Abingdon Press, 1966), 34.

19. Rudolph, *Frances Asbury*, 117.

20. Charles Grandison Finney, *Lectures on Revival of Religion* (New York: Levitt, Lord, and Company, 1835), 438.

21. Frank Greenville Beardsley, *Religious Progress through Religious Revivals* (New York: American Tract Society, 1943), 40; quoted by Roy J. Fish, *When Heaven Touched Earth* (Azle, TX: Need of the Times Publishers, 1996), 24.

22. Fish, *When Heaven Touched Earth*, 34.

23. Fish, *When Heaven Touched Earth*, 34.

24. William W. Sweet, *The Story of Religion in America* (New York: Harper and Brothers, 1930), 379.

25. This quote came from the author's notes in his PhD class under Dr. Roy Fish in a seminar titled "The History of Spiritual Awakenings."

26. J. Edwin Orr, *Good News in Bad Times* (Grand Rapids, MI: Zondervan Publishing House, 1953), 58.

27. Erling Jorstad, *That New-Time Religion* (Minneapolis, MN: Augsburg Publishing House, 1972), 37.

28. Michael Jacob, *Pop Goes Jesus* (New York: Morehouse-Barlow Company, 1972), 5.

29. Richard Ostling, Mayo Hohs, and Margaret Boeth, "The New Rebel Cry: Jesus Is Coming!," *Time* 97 (June 21, 1971): 59, 62.

30. Betty Price and Everett Hullam, "The Jesus Explosion," *Home Missions* (June/July 1971), 22.

31. Billy Graham, "The Marks of the Jesus Movement," *Christianity Today* 16 (November 5, 1971): 4–5.

32. C. H. Spurgeon, *Lectures to My Students* (Grand Rapids, MI: Zondervan, 1954), 33.

33. Charles Spurgeon, *Your Available Power* (New Kensington, PA: Whitaker, 1996), 13.

34. Henry Wadsworth Longfellow, "Outre-Mer: A Pilgrimage Beyond the Sea" (1833–1834).

35. C. S. Lewis, *God in the Dock: Essays on Theology and Ethics* (Grand Rapids, MI: Eerdmans, 1970), 61–62.

36. Jim Cymbala with Dean Merrill, *Fresh Wind, Fresh Fire* (Grand Rapids, MI: Zondervan, 1997). See pages 98–102 for a dramatic story of how the Prayer Band's intercession protected the pastor from a point-blank assault by a mentally disturbed gunman who disrupted a Sunday service.

37. Mark Waters, *The New Encyclopedia of Christian Quotations* (Grand Rapids, MI: Baker Books, 2000), 783.

38. George Atkins, "Brethren We Have Met to Worship," public domain.

39. Rudyard Kipling, "The Ballad of East and West," 1889.

40. Francis Thompson, in Francis Beauchesne Thornton, ed., *Return to Tradition: A Directive Anthology* (Milwaukee, WI: Bruce Publishing Co., 1948), 103ff.

41. J. B. Phillips, *The Young Church in Action* (New York: Macmillan, 1955), xvi.